MW00668731

Blessed

— BY THE —

Tongue

The Power Of The Word

Transform Your Vocabulary, Transform Your Life

Receive Joy

REDISCOVER TRUTH

Though the information contained within these pages is researched and documented, this is intended as a reference book for educational purposes only. The information is *not* intended to prescribe treatment or *cure* conditions. Further, any information brought fourth is *not* intended as medical advice *nor* intended to be used in place of medical treatment. The intent is merely the sharing of knowledge and information from the personal research and experience of the author. The reader is strongly encouraged to do further research. If medical challenges are prevalent and persist, please consult your doctor. You are highly encouraged to make your own health care decisions, based upon your own research, along with your health care professional. You are completely responsible for your own self if you choose to do anything based on the awareness you have gained within these pages.

Blessed By The Tongue:
The Power of the Word
Transform Your Vocabulary, Transform Your Life
By Receive Joy

Receive Joy Publishing
Naples, Florida, U.S.A.

© 2021 Receive Joy
Carisa Jones, Sylvia Lehmann
All rights reserved.
Cover art by IMCorp, LLC ©2020

ISBN: 978-0-9988484-6-4

Receive Joy, LLC
www.receivejoy.com
ask@receivejoy.com

DEDICATION

This book is dedicated to the Trinity:
God, Jesus, and The Holy Spirit.

CONTENTS

"In the beginning was the word. And the word was with God and **the word** was God."

—John 1:1 (NIV)

ABOUT *BLESSED BY THE TONGUE*

The authors of this book choose to speak only beautiful truth—or remain silent. We thank God for providing everything before we even know of our desires. And we thank Jesus for His complete work on the cross when He paid for everything in full and it truly is finished. Everything is a "gift from God, lest any man boast" (Ephesians 2:8-9). God is the gift and the giver. In the Spirit, we are complete. To manifest anything into the physical, all we have to do is to believe, master our speech, declare our askings, and receive our inheritance by being the matching vibration.

We are standing on the shoulders of all the great teachers that came before us: Jesus, Florence Scovel Shinn, Napoleon Hill, Anthony Robbins, Andrew Wommack, Louise Hay, Dr. Caroline Leaf, Dr. Norman Vincent Peale, Dr. Masaru Emoto, Hans Jenny, Reinhard Bonnke, Lynne McTaggart, ...

Some of these great humans mentioned transformational vocabulary, positive speaking, and the vibration of words before; however, we are here to go one step further to connect the dots and make you aware that:

- ♥ what you sow from your mouth is what you reap in your life: everything that is sent out comes back by the law of attraction,

- ♥ words are vibration,

- ♥ every single word you speak creates: What you say is exactly what you receive,

- ♥ it matters what we speak and listen to,

- ♥ you shall control your words, thoughts, and deeds,

- ♥ positive speaking is more than having a pleasant demeanor and pleasing personality: We have to be aware of the very words and phrases we use consciously and subconsciously, in our self-talk and internal dialog, silent thoughts in the form of words repeating themselves in our head, and surely the words we speak to ourselves and others, and

- ♥ when you master your tongue, you master your life.

This book explains:

- ♥ That words are creative energy and every word matters
- ♥ That God set up the Power of the Word before the beginning of time and left us *The Holy Bible* full of instructions on how to realize, acknowledge, and utilize this power.
- ♥ Why you shall be aware of your thoughts and words
- ♥ How to master your speech and take charge of your words
- ♥ How to build a transformational vocabulary to live by design
- ♥ How to be a God-trader and voice-activate your desires
- ♥ How to consciously create
- ♥ How to ask to receive
- ♥ Why we shall retire certain words and phrases, stop joking, and refrain from repeating sad stories
- ♥ How to journal
- ♥ How to pray into the solution
- ♥ How to use beautiful, positive affirmations
- ♥ The difference between listening and hearing
- ♥ How to bless with your tongue and speak life

With Love and Gratitude,

Receive Joy

INTRODUCTION

Look up. Look up at the sky. We see the blue. It is wonderfully vast. There is so much more out there than what is underneath our feet and immediately around us, even beyond what we can perceive with our eyes. There is more in the atmosphere than the air we breathe. There is an in-visible force that surrounds all. There is a Power. The Universe is full of Power.

We all agree that there is something powerful, tremendous, awesome, and mysterious out there which is greater than our self and part of our self. It is outside of us and it is inside of us. And although we may sometimes feel we are separate from it, we are indeed connected to it. As it surrounds us, it literally fills every cell and the space between them. It fills all matter.

We all come from this Power and are part of it. It is greater than our individual self. It is formulated from love. It contains all light and life. It is magnificent, it is free, and it is equally available to all of us. It provides continual abundance. It supports and embraces all life. Somehow, we have an inner knowledge that we are from this vast Heavenly Power containing continual awesome perfection.

This Power is a beautiful energy that exists and is full of absolute intelligence. It is consistent and flows continuously and progressively. Let us first connect to this Divine Power so that we can fully access and call on it.

This Power is called by many names. We call this Divine Power Source God, because it is so wonderful to know this source of light as a loving parental persona. Thus, we are lovingly drawn to develop and maintain an intimate relationship with Him.

God's Power is activated by the vibration of the Word.

Please read this book with an open heart and open mind. The following pages are written with the heart-filled intent to return to you the reins of your life through awareness.

Chapter 1

WORDS CREATE

How important are the words coming out of your mouth? We have all heard the saying:

What you say is what you get.

I shall add to that phrase by stating:

*What you **say** is **exactly**
what you will **receive**.*

This is the only possibility. The words we think, write, and speak are what we receive. And please know that **the spoken and/or written word trumps the thought**.

Being a magnetic force, humans attract consciously and subconsciously with the frequencies we transmit via our tongues, minds, and hearts. Creation of all kinds is activated when we use words. Since the human mind is so busy and our thoughts tend to be scattered, it is a blessing that the formulated word performs the final creation. **The thought attracts and the word creates.**

You create what **you speak** about. You speak about what you think of. You become what you think about most. Thus, edit your thoughts and your words. Think and speak about what you really wish for yourself and your life. Own your words.

Start by being aware of your words. Only speak out loud exactly what you desire to communicate. **Choose the words you speak with care.** It is vital to master your tongue.

At a seminar, I had the privilege to walk across hot coals. And even though my mind knew they were hot and my body was questioning my mind, I successfully crossed the coals because of my chanting and anchoring positive words: "Yes, I can. Cool moss. Cool moss. I am walking on cool moss." When my mind questioned the ability of my body to achieve it, my words trumped my thoughts.

Our words are an extension of us. Words are vibrational forces spiraling out from us and returning as solidified evidence (produced by each word) in the lives of their creators.

4

Each of our words are spirit-filled and life-giving. Once we speak them out loud or write them down, they become filled with life. Our physical world is a world of crystallized and solidified thoughts and words.

Swiss doctor and natural scientist Hans Jenny chronicled his observations on the power of sound vibrations in his 1967 book *Cymatics*. In his experiments, Jenny found sound vibrations have the power to create visual patterns in liquids, pastes, and powders.

Vibration is the force that moves us. Everything in existence vibrates. We are vibrational beings and we communicate with vibrational words. Our words vibrate, creating resonance, which forms energy. **Words themselves are energy. Energy is vibration and vibrations form life, light, and sound. Therefore, words create—literally!**

Our word vibrations have an immediate impact on the physical world around us. We know our world is constantly changing, and water is the first to recognize change. Water registers and reflects any frequency to which it is exposed.

Masaru Emoto, PhD, spent his life researching and educating humanity about water's true nature, and the effect our words and all vibrations have on water. His incredible water crystal photography demonstrates to our amazement how our thoughts, words, emotions, prayers, and music are truly vibrations that actually change the structure of water.

Dr. Emoto's legacy involved freezing water samples, after they had been exposed to various vibrational frequencies, to see if they formed into beautiful crystals or showed the absence of molecular structure, almost resembling mud. According to Dr. Emoto's tests, when a vial of water was labeled with a beautiful word, such as "love," "gratitude," "happiness," or "thank you" in a variety of languages, the water in the vial froze into perfect beautiful snowflakes, with every word forming a unique crystal. Continually, the positive words froze into beautiful crystal structures and all *negative* words froze without structure, lacking form or beauty. Dr. Emoto proved to the world that positive words hold beautiful creation power and are in tune with nature. *Negative* words lack beautiful creation power and these words and thoughts also have a chance to eliminate the beautiful crystals formed from even the purest water source.

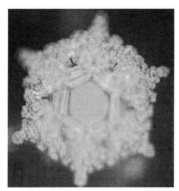

"Love and Gratitude"

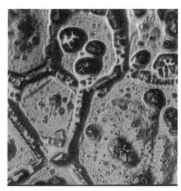

"You're stupid" spoken
repeatedly to water

"Happiness"

"Unhappiness"

"I can do it"

"I can't do it"

Chapter 2

GOD'S WORD

Let us rediscover the truth of the Word. God left us the gift of *The Holy Bible.* It is a book which, when opened, is full of only one thing: **words**. *The Bible* is our manual to this life experience. Every year, it is the number one bestselling book in the world. It supersedes all other book sales by such a great margin because humankind's powerful and universal desire to know God and His Word is continual.

Let us look at what *The Holy Bible* says about the power of our tongue and the words we speak:

James 3:5 reminds us that the **tongue** is a small part and **boasts great things**.

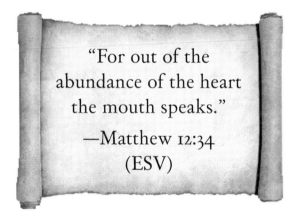

"For out of the abundance of the heart the mouth speaks."

—Matthew 12:34 (ESV)

"Death and **life** are **in** the power of **the tongue:** and they that love it shall eat the fruit thereof."

—Proverbs 18:21 (KJV)

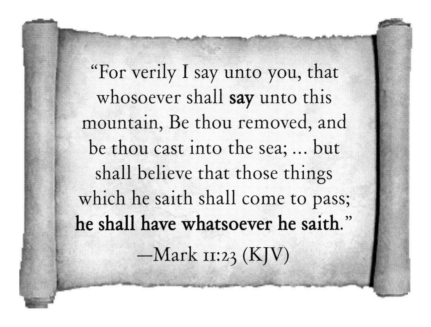

"For verily I say unto you, that whosoever shall **say** unto this mountain, Be thou removed, and be thou cast into the sea; ... but shall believe that those things which he saith shall come to pass; **he shall have whatsoever he saith.**"

—Mark 11:23 (KJV)

Death and life are in the power of our tongue and we shall have whatsoever we say. Wow! Let us take a moment to ponder this.

Have we ever been trained to lend attention to the exact words flowing out of our lips? Do we watch our words? Do we relay the truth? In *The Bible* it says:

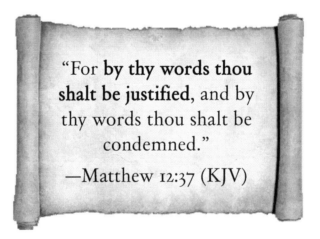

"For **by thy words thou shalt be justified,** and by thy words thou shalt be condemned."

—Matthew 12:37 (KJV)

God **spoke** everything into existence: the past, present, and future. **He created the whole world with words.**

With the first words God spoke in *The Bible*, He spoke light into existence, and so it is. God spoke the sky, the land, the waters, vegetation, the sun and the moon, aquatic life, birds, and animals into existence. He created all this with His words. God even made a perpetual decree with the water that the seas shall stay within their boundaries. Then God spoke His plan for human beings and He made us in His image and likeness. He even went further with His words: He spoke a blessing upon us to "be fruitful and multiply" and to "fill the earth and govern it." And so it was.

"And God **said**, 'Let there be light,' and there was light."

—Genesis 1:3 (NIV)

"And God **said**, 'Let the water under the sky be gathered to one place, and let dry ground appear.' And it was so. God called the dry ground 'land,' and the gathered waters he called 'seas.' And God saw that it was good."

—Genesis 1:9-10 (NIV)

"Then God **said**, 'Let Us make men in Our image, according to Our likeness; **let them have dominion** over the fish of the sea, over the birds of the air, and over the cattle, over all the earth and over every creeping thing that creeps on the earth.'"

—Genesis 1:26 (NKJV)

We are His chosen creation, made by Him and blessed by Him. We are blessed by His tongue (Genesis 1:28). What a great example of how we can also use our tongue: to bless.

In the Old Testament of *The Bible*, Moses asked God "Who shall I say You are?"

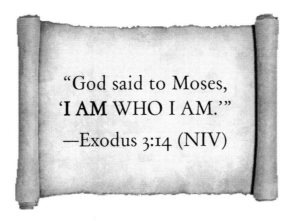

"God said to Moses,
'**I AM** WHO I AM.'"
—Exodus 3:14 (NIV)

In the New Testament, Jesus is called **THE WORD**.

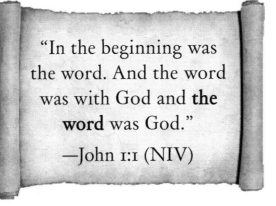

"In the beginning was the word. And the word was with God and **the word** was God."
—John 1:1 (NIV)

"**The Word became flesh** and made his dwelling among us. We have seen his glory, the glory of the one and only Son, who came from the Father, full of grace and truth."
—John 1:14 (NIV)

With the exception of forming humankind, God spoke everything that is into existence. God Himself uses words. All creation was, is, and will be spoken or written into existence. In John 1:1, God makes it very clear where creation power is. He is "**I AM**" and He is "**THE WORD**." God's power is in The Word.

Jesus changed matter and healed with his words:

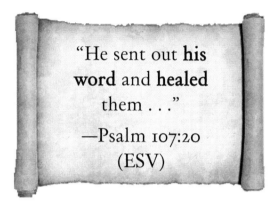

"He sent out **his word** and **healed** them . . ."

—Psalm 107:20 (ESV)

Jesus commanded everything into existence. **He** also **healed with words**. The promise Jesus left us with in John 14:12 is that we can do the same and even greater things than His works here on Earth.

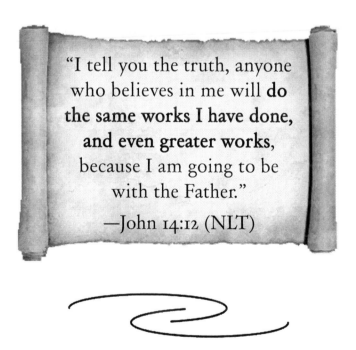

"I tell you the truth, anyone who believes in me will **do the same works I have done, and even greater works,** because I am going to be with the Father."

—John 14:12 (NLT)

Chapter 3

BE AWARE OF YOUR WORDS

I am justified (made right in God's sight) by the words of my mouth!

Mark 11:23 says when you desire to move a mountain, all you have to do is **speak**, and when you **BELIEVE WHAT YOU SAY**, then you can **receive** your desired outcome.

How do we start believing what we say? First, we shall **start listening** to—and thus hearing—what we are saying.

Jesus reminded us to be careful of what we hear, because what we **hear** will be multiplied unto us:

> "Therefore consider carefully how you **listen**. Whoever has will be given more;"
>
> —Luke 8:18 (NIV)

> "So then faith comes by **hearing**, and hearing by the word of God."
>
> —Romans 10:17 (NKJV)

Hearing, according to *The Bible,* **means to understand**. We are taking in the information and absorbing it, making it part of our belief system, and thus our faith. Our understanding comes from what we hear; spoken by others, by ourselves, and by our internal voice. When we hear, we gain understanding from the sounds to which we have been listening. (Today's word agreement seems reversed. Most people define hearing as the faculty of receiving sounds. To listen is to give attention to sounds.)

Train yourself to hear/understand life-giving words and receive the goodness of life multiplied unto you. When you hear the woes of the world, you have zero as a multiplier. Everything multiplied by zero remains zero. Please consider the multiplicative Power of positive Words when you think them, write them, speak them, and hear them.

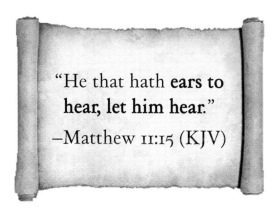

"He that hath **ears to hear, let him hear**."
–Matthew 11:15 (KJV)

Words produce faith—both good or the opposite—all depending on the exact words. **Believe the Word of God.**

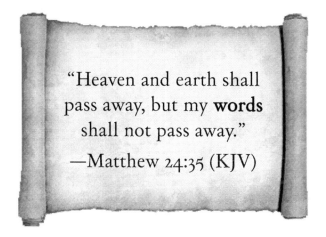

"Heaven and earth shall pass away, but my **words** shall not pass away."
—Matthew 24:35 (KJV)

God's **Word will remain and endure forever**. What about our words?

Hear the exact words formed by your tongue and coming forth from your own mouth and ask yourself:

♥ Am I conscious and aware of my own words?

♥ Are my words positive and encouraging?

♥ Am I encouraging myself and others with every word I speak?

♥ Are my words a blessing?

♥ Are my words reassuring, loving and healing?

♥ Are my words defining me?

♥ How do my words come to me?

♥ Who influenced my vocabulary?

♥ Is my vocabulary from God's Word calling forth victory?

♥ When I learned to talk, were people around me aware of the power of every word?

♥ Do I understand the power of my own words?

♥ Do I know that every word matters because words move matter?

♥ Do I know that my words create?

♥ What are the consequences of my current speech?

Notes

I once had a salesperson come to my house to demonstrate a piece of equipment in which I was interested. She said that the equipment is so good that she does "*not need*" to sell it to me, she is just here to share the greatness of it. I replied, "Wow! This is interesting. Then I will have to call someone else, because I am ready to buy this piece of equipment." She thought for a moment and said, "Oh, what I really mean is, I am happy to sell it to you. That is what I am here for." I advised her to declare her desired outcome by choosing her words carefully.

When I followed up with her a couple months later, she and her business partner told me sales were up. They had been wondering why they had so many people showing interest in the product, yet sales were lower than expected. They were asking for the reason when the salesperson met me. This was a huge "aha" moment when **they first became conscious of the words they were using** to sell their product, and what they were teaching in their sales trainings. Changing their words made a big difference and increased their closing rate significantly.

Watch your mind and your tongue. Why shall you desire to control the words coming from your mouth? Because the words spoken by your mouth create your life and influence your happiness, health, and wealth. When you learn this one fact, your life will transform to its greatness.

Your words **give life**. They set the tone and pattern for your being. They breathe life into every moment and situation. When your repetitive speech patterns (or "self-talk"/ internal dialog) are joyful and uplifting, your day and life will be so much better.

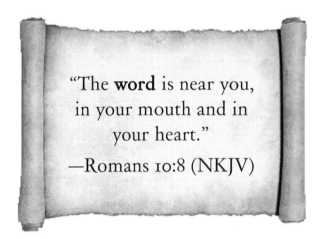

"The **word** is near you,
in your mouth and in
your heart."
—Romans 10:8 (NKJV)

Your mouth holds the ability to speak words, accept, ask, declare, call forth, confess faith, pray, petition, express gratitude, preach, encourage, sing, praise, worship, heal, repent, and bless.

Chapter 4

YOUR WORDS CREATE YOUR LIFE

God's word gave us dominion over the Earth. **How do we hold this dominion? With our belief and our words.** Because we are the children of God, we share His creation power. Humans are the only creatures on Earth that are able to speak words. This grants us the unique ability to **co-create with God.** We are His greatest creation and we are made in His image. Because He creates, we can create, and He creates by **speaking things into existence.** We shall be aware that we have as much power to create the positive as the opposite. When God spoke, he always created that which was "good" and "very good." Are we aware enough of our words so that we also create that which is "good" and "very good"? Let us use our vocabulary to always say what we really mean in order to create what is good.

All things are ours already. Yet, to bring them into manifestation, we shall declare and verbally profess them into the physical world.

God told Adam to name every animal on Earth. God certainly had the ability to name everything Himself and yet He had the desire to interact and co-create with Adam right from the beginning and now with all humanity. God chose humans to co-create the specifics of our environment with Him and encouraged us to **use our words** to do it. At that moment humans went from thinking in images to thinking and communicating about those images with words. Words are symbols on whose meanings people have agreed.

The words used by us and those around us establish and affect our own set of beliefs about who we are and what our life is and shall become. Our vocabulary shapes and defines who we are. Please be aware that our **repetitive words** constantly **shape our life**. Like God, we create with the use of our words. Let us be consciously aware of the words we choose to use.

Our words come from our thoughts. When we simply listen to our own words, we can tell how positive our thoughts are in every moment.

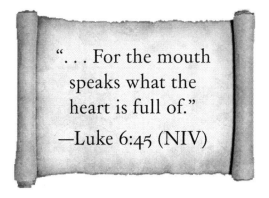

"... For the mouth speaks what the heart is full of."

—Luke 6:45 (NIV)

Speaking positive words begins with keen awareness, followed by positive thinking and a kind heart. We are reminded in Matthew 12:34 that out of the abundance of the heart the mouth speaks. Our words can represent the good treasures we have stored up within. *The Bible* also reminds us that our words are proceeding from our heart. They show forth our heart.

Life is in the power of the tongue (Proverbs 18:21). Please realize what God is saying to us about the power of words. Make a conscious choice to speak of the things that are honest, just, pure, lovely, of good report, and have virtue and praise as suggested in Philippians 4:8:

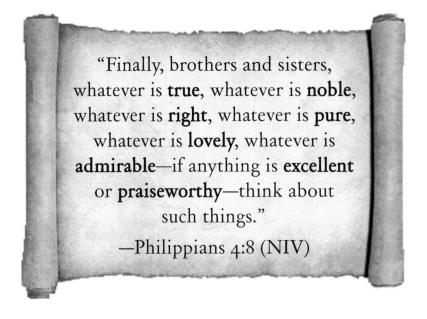

"Finally, brothers and sisters, whatever is **true**, whatever is **noble**, whatever is **right**, whatever is **pure**, whatever is **lovely**, whatever is **admirable**—if anything is **excellent** or **praiseworthy**—think about such things."

—Philippians 4:8 (NIV)

Ask God to renew your mind and help you gain awareness of your words. Practice rightmindedness. **Control your thoughts and your speech.** When necessary, adjust or correct them. Think positively, speak positively, act positively, listen to positive messages, and befriend truly positive people. What have you been doing up to this point? Choose positivity right now. Open and renew your heart and your mind and **be blessed by your tongue.** Ask God to receive your blessing in this area of your life. Begin now: take a vow to speak positively. Read the following prayer out loud:

> Dear Heavenly Father, please renew my heart and my mind. As of this moment, I will only think encouraging and positive thoughts and speak positive words. I use my tongue to bless this world and everyone in it. I go forth in 100% confidence. I am healthy. I will call in all the Divine greatness that You, God, have stored up for me since the beginning of time. I renounce my illusionary free will and welcome in Your perfect Divine Will for my life that was set up from the foundation of the world.

Our words create our reality. Often, our yet-to-be-trained mouth can give *negativity* temporary authority over us. Control your tongue and live a victorious life. Speak out loud and call in your bright future. **We reap the fruits of our ideas and our words.** When we live confidently in faith and are connected to the light of God, our words show it.

The choice of our words does matter when we use them to talk to ourselves and other beings. Every word matters. Matter changes to match our words. **Transform your vocabulary** and in doing so **transform your life!**

Chapter 5

EVERY WORD MATTERS

Because our words have the power to bless (or the opposite) let us decide to make every word count. Tame and train your tongue. This entails bringing the common words and phrases we use all the time to our awareness, allowing us to change every word to a blessing. Let us convert them into positive creations. Let us be conscious of what we are calling in and expressing with our exact words in every moment. Remember to bring your attention to your words and what comes out of your mouth.

Let us now talk about the principles of controlling our tongues. **The answer to a new, more vibrant life is in your mouth**; creation power is in your tongue.

To use the language of the Universe, we have to always, in every instance, speak into the solution (speak the solution into existence) by using positive, declarative, empowering words, phrases, and sentences.

The use of "*no,*" "*not,*" "*nothing,*" "*never,*" "*don't,*" "*can't,*" "*haven't,*" "*isn't,*" "*wouldn't,*" "*shouldn't,*" and "*couldn't*" takes us away from our original intent and brings the focus to that which we actually prefer to let go of. With these thoughts and words, we are confusing and scrambling our co-creation power. When we use these words, we are declaring the opposite of what we truly wish to accomplish. Change "*isn't*" to **is** (am, be), "*don't*" to **do,** and "*haven't*" to **have**. Let us state everything in present tense. There is only the present moment. I once heard a riddle that asked, "What do a prince and a pauper have in common?" Answer: "The present moment." And it is what we decide to do with this present moment that determines whether we are the prince or the pauper. Creation power is only available in the present moment.

We use a lot of words and phrases that were handed to us habitually. When we take a moment and really think about what we just said, we are oftentimes surprised by the true meaning these words hold.

For example, when we say that we will "*unleash* our power," it suggests to the Universe that it has to create a "leash" in order to fulfill our thought or command to be "*unleashed*." Similarly, "*unstoppable*" suggests one may currently be "stopped," and when we are flowing, the Universe now has an order to "stop" us first.

This theory reveals that we spend a lot of time creating things to "*un*"-create. It lacks efficiency, uses double the effort, and creates confusion. This is like running away from the finish line when our original intention is to run toward it. **Be mindful of using words starting with "*un-*" and also words containing "*-less*."** Also, be aware of using "*not*" similarly to "*un-*," as with "*unsure*" or "*not* sure" and "*unavailable*" or "*not* available."

Even when positive words are used in phrases, combined they may create the opposite of what you really intend to say and create. "Running in circles" strung together has a meaning we wish to stay away from, whereas "running" and "circles" have good word agreements. "Work" is a good thing, "hard" is a desired state for molecules; however, "work hard" strikes an emotion and may change our vibration.

In today's language, we use a lot of **double negatives** attempting to state the positive outcome. We say for example, "*no problem*," "*not bad*," "*it isn't over*," "*I won't forget*," "*it can't get worse*," "*no trouble at all*," or "*it can't go wrong*." Remember, when we use zero as a multiplier, the creative sum is still zero.

To state your intentions in the positive, ask yourself: What do I really mean? What do I desire to accomplish sending forth these words? What is my desired outcome?

For every statement to go straight to the finish line, we shall omit words that point us in the opposite direction, such as "*without*" and "_____-*free*."

Two phrases used too often are "*don't worry*" and "*no worries*." Why do we desire to create "*worry*" in order "*not to*"? Think about the phrase, "You are *never* going to believe this..." What do we really mean? That God blessed us in our circumstances, and it is so miraculous that we wish to tell about it. Let us start the conversation with "You will absolutely like what I am about to tell you" or "God is so miraculous" or "This great thing just happened to me." We clearly use sayings even though they lack positivity and efficiency. We use them out of habit, laziness, confusion, and desire to blame. We have learned to babble automatic responses, and we habitually insert them into our speech. Hopefully, you have now learned that the results we call in may be the opposite of what we desire to call in. When anyone hands us words that lack blessing or may lower our personal positivity, respond with blessed uplifting words. For example, "Yes, may God continue to bless me and you!" or "Have a nice day!"

When I first came to the United States for an internship position and learned English, I was very impressed with the positive replies I received when I offered someone a "thank you." There were warm smiles and phrases, such as "my pleasure" and "you are welcome." Being born in Berlin, Germany, where eye contact and kindness was rather rare, I felt very welcomed, and these responses quickly became also a habit in my vocabulary. When I returned home to study in northern Germany, I made being welcoming and nice to everyone a priority that surely received recognition and trained me well for my service on cruise ships. I am grateful that I learned in my early twenties that I have a choice in the words I use and the demeanor with which I present them. After eight years, I came back to Florida and noticed that the responses to "thank you" have changed. Now, I am frequently handed "*no problem*," "*no worries*," and "I *don't blame* you." What happened to our language? I certainly pray for a revival of positive manners and positive word choices. This is the reason I advocate for the Power of Positive Words.

Be aware of words you speak over your own life and what you attract with them. Think about it. To be a "*warrior* for peace," the Universe will help to find a "*battle*" for you to "*war*" in. Another phrase we use is "the sky is the *limit*." Is the sky *limited*? Having "*unlimited* power" suggests a *limit* as well. Let us confess to be "advocates of peace" and dream as "vast as the sky" with "absolute power."

> *Ask yourself: What words and phrases can I change or improve? What exactly do I now choose to change them to?*

_____

_____

_____

_____

_____

_____

_____

_____

_____

When God created in the first page of *The Bible*, He said all that He created is "good," meaning absolutely perfect for the purpose for which it was created. How brilliant! We humans tend to say "*not bad*" when what we really mean is the opposite. God uses proper words to say what He means. Let us follow His example.

Let us consciously empower our life by **transforming our vocabulary**. Every word we choose creates something. Let us start by looking at **common words and phrases we may repetitively be using and their new and improved, creative alternatives**.

Below is a list of examples of commonly used phrases of which to become consciously aware and creative options to enhance your vocabulary, and hence your creation power. For a far more extensive list, please refer to the back pages of this book (69-109) where we have compiled words and phrases over many years of listening to peoples' word choices.

TRANSFORMATIONAL VOCABULARY: PHRASES

ADVANCED AWARENESS	CREATIVE CHOICE
A deal you can't refuse	A deal you will absolutely wish to accept
A method behind the madness	Using strategy
A price to pay	Consequences
A woman's work is never done	A woman's work blesses everyone
Absolutely unreal	It was absolutely amazing; magical
An awful lot/An infinite number of	An abundance of
As good as it gets	This is perfect; I am satisfied with this
At last/At least	Finally; yes; I'm so pleased/happy
Bad idea	Let's come up with a better idea
Bad luck	A super challenge; I'm wide open to a better fortune
Bad news	Be aware; different expectation
Better safe than sorry	Be careful; be prepared
Can't get any better	This is perfection
Come to your senses	Wake up
Debt free	Financially sound; everything is paid in full
Didn't miss anything	Captured everything
Do you mind	Will you please
Doing nothing	Relaxing; simply being
Don't forget/I won't forget	Remember/I'll remember
Don't make the mistake of	Be certain; use caution
Don't worry	Be happy; be encouraged; take heart
Don't be so hard on yourself	Love yourself
Don't beat yourself up	Love yourself; own your life

ADVANCED AWARENESS	CREATIVE CHOICE
Don't bother	All is well; let it be; I am fine
Don't get me wrong	What I am really saying here
Don't make excuses	Just do it
Don't make the mistake of	Be certain
Don't panic	Stay calm
Don't procrastinate	Motivate yourself; just do it; take action now
Don't settle for less	Go for more; be certain
Easier said than done	This currently challenges me; I will rise to the occasion
Falling in love	Welcoming in love
Fat/Fighting chance	A possibility
For God's/Heaven's sake	For goodness sake; oh my goodness
Get ahead	Advance; prosper; become more
Getting worse	More challenging
God forbid	Even when _____
God only knows why	It is beyond me
Good luck	I super believe in you
Greatest fear	I feel in my heart that _____
Hard work/Work hard	I gave that a lot of energy
Hard-earned/Hard-fought	Well-earned; valuable
Hate to miss it	I will be with you in spirit; I prefer to be there
Hopefully there's no _____	I declare _____
How bad can it be/get	The fact of the matter is _____
I can't help it/I can't explain it	I am compelled to do it
I can't afford it	I really wish to have _____

ADVANCED AWARENESS	CREATIVE CHOICE
I can't wait	I am so excited; I am looking forward to; I am ready
I couldn't believe _____	It surprised me
I don't blame you	I agree
I don't like/I don't want _____	I prefer _____
I refuse to _____	I choose to _____
I refuse to believe that _____	I choose to believe _____
I wish I could	I am looking at possibilities; I desire to; I can
I wouldn't complain	I am pleased/satisfied
I'm confused	I desire clarity/understanding
I'm in a hurry	I have a lot to accomplish right now
I'm sick of always/It's a pain to always	I prefer to _____; I rather _____
I'm starving	I feel so hungry
If you have not already	Will you; can I ask a favor of you
Impossible situation	A situation beyond me; God help
In God's timing	Now; miraculously
It can't/couldn't hurt	Let's try; it helps
It doesn't matter	It's alright
It will blow your mind	It will expand your mind
It's a shame	I prefer; I wish
It's no accident	It's by design
It's no secret	It's common knowledge
It's not fool-proof	Be aware
It's not your fault	You allowed _____
It's so hard/Life's hard	It's currently challenging

ADVANCED AWARENESS	CREATIVE CHOICE
Knock yourself out	Go for it; do your best
Last, but not least	One more thing; the last important item is _____
Learn to accept it	Count it all joy; create better
Less is more	Simplify
Less pain	Feel good/well
Less stress	Calm; at peace
Like it or not/Believe it or not	Like it and enjoy it
Lose weight	My ideal weight is _____
Lost cause	God help
Make it happen	Allow God's grace
Make no mistake	My point is _____
Midlife crisis	New greatness; a new chapter in my life
More or less	Almost; pretty much
My bad	I am responsible; sorry
My phone is dead/dying	My phone has to be charged
My worst nightmare	My greatest challenge; my deepest desire
Needless to say	Obviously
Never a dull moment	Always full of excitement
Never enough	Always ready to receive more; room for more
Never fails	Always happens; consistently
Never forget	Always remember; promise to remember
Never give up/let go/stop	Stay the course; persevere; hold on
Never too late	Now is a good time to _____
No clue/Don't know	Yet to know
No doubt	Absolutely; of course; for sure; I agree

ADVANCED AWARENESS	CREATIVE CHOICE
No matter what	By all means; for sure
No nonsense	Straightforward
No one is perfect/We all have our faults	We are perfect as we are; God made us as we are
No pain	Feel great; perfect health; restored
No problem/Not a problem	It's my pleasure; you are welcome; blessings
No worries	Be happy; I'm happy to do this for you
Not a bad idea	That's actually a good idea
Not too long ago	Recently
Not too shabby/Not bad at all	Looks good
Not yet	Yet to be; soon
Nothing to be afraid of/Nothing to fear	All is good; all is well; there is only God's grace
Nothing wrong with it	It is perfect; it is alright
Nothing wrong with you	You are great; you are healthy
Out of luck/No such luck	Imagine something better; let's turn things our way
Plan of attack	Victorious plan; detailed plan
Problem-free	solution-oriented
Rather be safe than sorry	Be prepared
Regardless of/Despite	Anyway
Same old	Once again; repeated; familiar
Should not _____	I prefer _____
Sick and tired	Ready to advance
Solving problems	Creating solutions; solution-oriented
Something is wrong	Something is off

ADVANCED AWARENESS	CREATIVE CHOICE
Suffer the consequences	Experience variety; actions create consequences
That is not our problem	The temporary challenge is _____
That was dumb	That was something
That's too bad	It's getting better and better
The sky is the limit	Everything is possible; the possibilities are wide open; vast as the sky
The worst part was	The most concerning part was
There is no end/limit to it	There is a great amount of; it is continuous
There is no room for mistakes	Please be precise
They don't understand/No one gets me	I believe in myself
This is to die for	This is wonderful
This sucks	I desire _____; I prefer _____
Time is money	Time is valuable
Time will heal all wounds	Have faith and joyfully let go; let God
Too good to be true	Wondrous; miraculous; amazing
Too late	Life is progressing according to plan
Tough break	I experienced contrast
Unconditional love	Perfect love; pure love; agape love
Undeniable truth	Absolute truth; proven truth
Under the circumstances	In this situation
Under the gun	Focus and finish
Under the weather	Please rest; I allow myself to stay home and rest
Undivided attention	Complete attention
Unlimited potential	Vast potential

ADVANCED AWARENESS	CREATIVE CHOICE
We are in luck	Miracles are real; God's favor is on me; thanks God
We won't take no for an answer	Please say yes
Weighed down	Overpowered
Weight loss	My ideal weight is _____
What a coincidence	What a coordinated manifestation; divine order; serendipity
What is the problem/trouble	How may I help
When in doubt	When you have questions
Without a doubt	Sure; certain
Without further delay	Now; immediately, right away
Without question	Absolutely
Worst enemy	It's all me
Worst-case scenario	Less than favorable; least desirable
Worth fighting for	Of great value
You are fooling yourself	You have high hopes
You are merely	You are
You are never going to believe this/You won't believe what _____	I am really excited to share this with you; this just happened; I really have to tell you about _____
You can't lose	You can only win
You can't miss it	You will definitely see it
You don't understand	Please understand; allow me to explain
You have no idea	It was amazing; please understand
You never know	There is always a possibility

 Do you use some of the listed expressions in your daily vocabulary? Highlight the phrases you use often.

"For, 'Whoever would love life and see good days must **keep their tongue** from evil and their lips **from deceitful speech.**'"

—1 Peter 3:10 (NIV)

Carefully listen to the words and phrases we use and the words everyone around us uses. Start practicing alternate positive words until they become a new, wonderful habit.

Let us always be consciously aware of our words. Let us train ourselves to clean up our words and **edit ourselves** continuously. In doing this we magnetically attract so many new good things into our lives. Editing upfront ensures accurate creation.

"Let your **conversation** be **gracious** and **attractive** so that you will have the right response for everyone."

—Colossians 4:6 (NLT)

A few years ago, my children gave me a plaque for Christmas with a common saying on it: "*Don't worry* about tomorrow, God is already there." The first thing I did was place a new phrase over the first two words: "Be inspired."

It sat on my desk for over a month before I realized two more necessary corrections. We live in a series of **present moments** and we ask our God to be **here** with us **today**. With this second change, the plaque now declares: "Be inspired about today, God is always here."

> Take the next two weeks and be aware of the words you use repetitively.
>
> Make a list and then ask yourself: What words can I change to improve my outcome?

We can literally change our experience by using better words. *Negative* thoughts and speech often cancel the miracles you previously created with God. Thus, be aware of and edit your words. Clear the path and keep it clear. Adjust your compass to your true north (the solution) and head straight there. Head north with your tongue vibrationally. Are your words in alignment with your desires? Align your thoughts and the words you speak. Say what you really mean so the right vibration is sent out and will return to you. Train your mind by training your vocabulary and your life will begin to match what you are saying. Direct your words to the desired solution.

When my 91-year-old friend and yoga instructor was ready to live in a nursing home, we went through all his important documents. He chose me to be executor of his will. I talked with him about his long-term insurance policy and asked him to tell me the story of when he bought it. His words were, "The salesperson told me that I will most likely *never* use it, *but* it is good to have anyway." He bought the policy and paid the annual premiums for 35 years, which amounted to roughly $350,000. The policy stated that in the case that the policyholder moves to a nursing home, the first 60 days rent will be paid by the policyholder before the insurance begins coverage. My friend passed on after 59 days in the nursing home. Our words endure forever.

Oftentimes, we speak greatness and cancel the creation in the same sentence when we use the word "*but*." Let us make sure that whatever follows after stays encouraging. "And" or "yet" are better choices. You may also use: although, however, on the other hand, still, and though. Also, change "*if*" to "when."

Words like "*could,*" "*should,*" "*would,*" "*maybe,*" and "*might*" represent a desire for things to be different and are waiting for concrete manifestation. While using these words we have yet to **call forth a definite command to declare a specific outcome**. These words are confusing for the Universe and instill a feeling of lacking resolution. To create with awareness, Receive Joy suggests you state what you truly desire using declarative statements, such as:

- ♥ I can _____
- ♥ I do _____
- ♥ I shall _____
- ♥ I choose _____
- ♥ I accept _____
- ♥ I allow _____
- ♥ I am _____
- ♥ I receive _____
- ♥ I am so grateful that (I have) _____

The Universe *"needs and wants for nothing."* **God's Universe already has and contains everything.** When you are *"trying," "going to get"* something or *"want"* something, the Quantum Field allows us to "keep on *trying," "trying to get,"* "keep *going and going,"* and *"wanting* and *wanting."* Let us move on from the *"wanting* state" and declare that everything is already here. The following lists contain powerful substitutions to use instead of *"want"* and *"need."*

For example, replace "I *want* to go on vacation" with "I **desire** a vacation," "I am **excited** about my upcoming vacation," or "I **fancy** a vacation."

Change "I *need* to *get* it done" to "I now **declare** this task complete."

POWERFUL WORD CHOICES TO DECLARE A DESIRE (*WANT*)

adequacy/adequate	hunger for
admiration for	inclined to
ambition	intend/intention
ask	like
aspire to/aspiration	long for
attracted to	longing
avidity	love
call forth	luxury
call in	motive/motivation
choice/choose	necessity
command	passion for
crave	please us
declare	pleasure
demand	pray
desire	prefer
eager to receive	pursue
embrace	relish
excited to	require
fancy	seek
fascination	thirst for
fervor	urge for
fondness	welcome
hankering	welcome in
have appetite for	will
have the will	wish for
hope	yearn for
hope for	

POWERFUL WORD CHOICES TO DECLARE A REQUIREMENT *(NEED)*

declare	beneficial
request	demand
require	right
necessity	use
essential	urge
have occasion for	wish

Retire the words on the following list completely as they attract less desired outcomes into our lives. Receive Joy encourages all humanity to omit these words and phrases from our casual vocabulary and replace them with positive words that hold creation power:

WORDS TO RETIRE

abuse	competition	doubt
accident	corrupt	doubtful
ageless	could	dread
anger	couldn't	dreadful
anxiety	crisis	enemy
at least	curse	evil
attack	cursed	fail
bad	damn	failure
badass	death	false ideas
battle	depression	fear
battlefield	despair	fearful
battling	desperate	fearless
blame	desperately	fight
bondage	despite	fool
bother	didn't	fool-proof
boundless	difficult	foolish
brain fog	difficulties	get
but	disaster	greed
can't	don't	grief

WORDS TO RETIRE

guilt	no matter	struggle
hate	not	stupid
hatred	or not	suffer
haven't	pain	terrible
heartbreak	panic	trouble
hell	pathetic	try
hellish	poor	ugly
hopeless	poverty	unabridged
ill	problem	unconditional
illness	procrastinate	unexpected
imprisoned	rage	unfortunately
imprisonment	reckless	unless
isn't	resent	unspoken
jealous	resentment	victim
jealousy	sabotage	war
judgement	scarcity	warrior
lack	separation	weapon
looser	shame	won't
luck	should	worry
mean	shouldn't	worse
misery	sick	worst
mistake	sickness	would
must	sin	wouldn't
never	sorrow	wrong
nevertheless	stress	
no	stressed-out	

For advanced awareness, Receive Joy also collected a more comprehensive list of words that shall be exchanged with creative word choices. Please refer to the back pages (110-118) of this book.

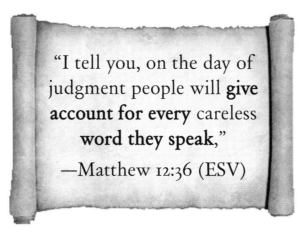

"I tell you, on the day of judgment people will **give account for every** careless **word they speak**,"

—Matthew 12:36 (ESV)

Our words create everything. Every word counts, in this lifetime and forevermore. Every word is a creation. We can choose to create love, joy, gratitude, hope, compassion, mercy, praise, and much more positivity with our words—or we can choose to create the lack thereof.

"So is **my word** that goes out from my mouth: It will not return to me empty, but **will** accomplish what I desire and **achieve the purpose for which I sent it**."

—Isaiah 55:11 (NIV)

Once an elderly gentleman came to my house and told me about his car accident from years ago. He offered to show me pictures of him injured. I invited him to show me pictures of all the good things in his life and explained to him that this will bring both of us greater joy. Better that the past remains in the past. Let us share our happy stories as well as our dreams and desires. We will still have plenty to talk about.

Let us also be conscious of **only sharing our happy stories**. Please refrain from telling the other stories. **Every time a story is retold, we are recreating it all over again and drawing it into the present**, thus fueling the past and attracting more of it. In other words, the *negative* fire is kindled. Ask yourself: Why am I repeating sad stories I best forget? Is it for significance, as an excuse, in defense, for fun, out of laziness, or to gain temporary rapport with others? Let us set all our sad stories down on God's altar for good. He is already well aware of all these details in our life. Let us be aware to only pass on the encouraging words and positive stories we wish to have imprinted in our mind and re-created in our life. Living by design starts by being aware of the stories we repeat. Let us hear and use our own positive, encouraging stories.

> "This they said, testing Him, that they might have something of which to accuse Him. But Jesus stooped down and **wrote on the ground with *His* finger, as though He did not hear.** So when they continued asking Him, He raised Himself up and said to them, 'He who is without sin among you, let him throw a stone at her first.' And again He stooped down and wrote on the ground."
> —John 8:6-8 (NKJ)

Stop all gossip.

Even more confusing are silly phrases such as "*holy cow,*" "*barking up the wrong tree,*" "*bite the bullet,*" and "*when pigs fly.*" Take a moment to think about them. What do the words of the phrases mean? The phrases have agreement with us that is deeply embedded in our culture. However, the words that make up these phrases have a completely different meaning. Are we using these phrases as fillers and out of habit and laziness, or simply to "hear ourselves talk"? Have we thought about them before they leave our mouth? What is the true meaning we wish to convey with these phrases? When we sent them forth out of our mouth what do we expect them to achieve? *The Bible* reminds us that every word we send out will come back answered (Isaiah 55:11).

When I was growing up, my parents often said to me, "*Don't* put every word on the golden scale" whenever I questioned their silly words. My inner being knew that **every word counts**. Now I understand what they really meant by using this saying. I learned to remain neutral to silly phrases, although now I comprehend that the whole Universe literally weighs and answers every word. I am thankful that I was gifted from childhood with a questioning awareness of the Power of the Word.

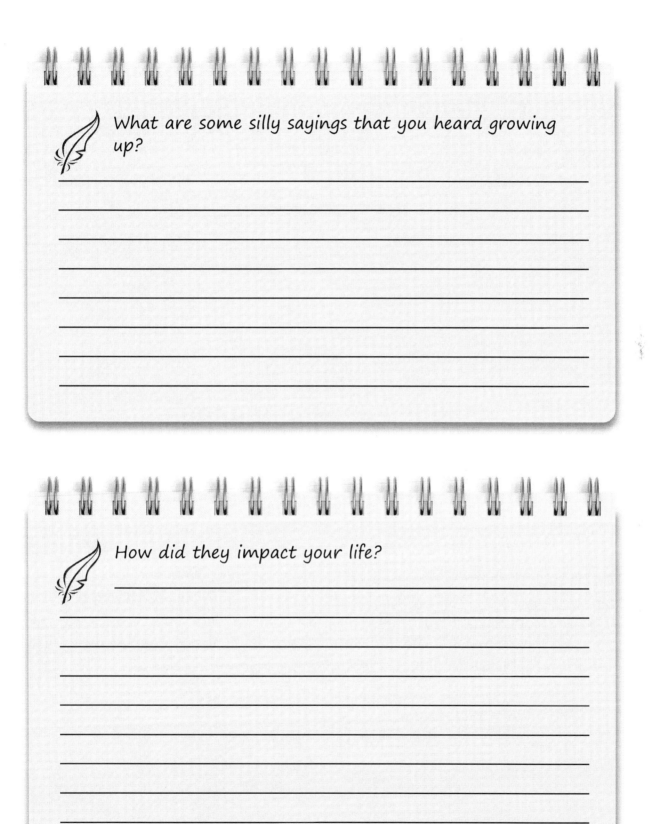

What are some silly sayings that you heard growing up?

_____

_____

_____

_____

_____

How did they impact your life?

_____

_____

_____

_____

_____

_____

Use new, empowering phrases to replace the old phrases!

_____

_____

_____

_____

_____

_____

_____

_____

Word choice awareness is also necessary when joking with our words, because our words are even then in creation mode. **Stop joking** in all forms: _jestering, smart-talking, kidding around, bantering, teasing, making fun of, mocking, gagging, wisecracking, smart-assing, fooling, using slang, petty criticizing, stirring up, cursing,_ and _provoking one another._ Especially think about the fact that we often joke with others about ourselves.

Set down your sad stories, stop joking, show gratitude, and **change all** your _negative_ **"babble" to positive blessings**. Happily continue to share funny stories and jokes that state, reinforce and create positive images and scenarios. Do **keep on smiling and laughing**! Laughter is pure and inspiring. Laugh with one another about things, situations, or clever twists rather than making fun of anyone. You may also choose to **hold your tongue and be still**.

When your vocabulary still contains "curse words," omit them.

> "Do you see a man who
> is **hasty in his words?**
> There is more hope for
> a fool than for him."
> —Proverbs 29:20 (ESV)

One of my favorite neighbors volunteered to co-chair a local charity event. Besides being asked to raise money, solicit sponsorships, and create collateral for the event, she was also assigned the task of collecting donations for a grand "winner-takes-all" raffle drawing. Over a period of eight months, she put her heart and soul into the project and personally collected more than $28,000 in gift certificates, services, and merchandise, ranging from a year of haircuts at a local salon, a six-hour appointment with a professional organizer, a diamond necklace, to a deluxe massage package and a complete car detailing for the drawing. Two days before the event, I went over to see how things were coming along and noticed that the gift baskets, bags, and boxes, previously contained to the guest room, had surprisingly taken over her entire condominium. When I pointed this out, my friend said, "In two days, it will all be gone and out of my home, and all I can say is; it better *not* come back." I became cognizant of the power of her words when a few days later, I saw all of the baskets, bags, and boxes piled up in the middle of her living room. Her mother, who had attended the event as her guest, had purchased nine raffle tickets and won the entire lot. In a state of shock, my friend and her mother loaded up their cars and brought everything back home. What she really meant to say was, "I am ready once again to enjoy my clean house" or "I am excited to have my house and space to myself again."

Let us speak clearly of what we invite in our lives. The Universe focuses on and reacts to words with powerful creation ability to provide, very specifically, what we are asking for. It sorts, processes, and eliminates other words. Our word choice might confuse the meaning of what we are trying to accomplish and may cause a reaction taking us in the complete opposite direction from our goal.

"Not what goes into the mouth defiles a man; but **what comes out of the mouth**, this defiles a man."

—Matthew 15:11 (NKJV)

Words are organized thoughts. They reveal what is on our minds and ultimately what is in our hearts. When our use of positive words requires further development, this may show that our thoughts yearn for conscious enhancement. Let us revitalize our thoughts. Choose positivity over what the movies, media, Internet, and news of the world offer us. How are these distractions shaping your internal world and dialog? Let us remember that all messages on which we focus hold the opportunity to affect us.

"**Let the words of my mouth,** and the meditation of my heart, **be acceptable in thy sight,** O LORD, my strength, and my redeemer."

—Psalm 19:14 (KJV)

Chapter 6

CONSIOUSLY CREATE WITH YOUR WORDS

Are your words supporting your purpose? Be conscious of which words you send out to truly achieve what you desire.

Our beautiful words are another way to increase our vibration. The words we speak have a physical impact on matter. When we reprogram our habitual speaking, we reprogram our thinking. This is why **repeatedly speaking positive affirmations enhances our lives. Changing our minds and beliefs, along with optimizing our words, will correct and bless the vibrations we emit to the Universe.** Our Universe has a perfect language, and when we speak this language we have beautiful communication power.

In the beginning was the Word. We can start using our creation power by discovering and **rediscovering all the good words** available to us, welcoming them in, and training our minds to use this expanded positive vocabulary. Let us always speak kind words of abundance. To some of us, it may feel like learning a new language. This new language is conscious creation. Let us extend our vocabulary. English is the language with the most words. We tend to use the same words and phrases over and over. Make it a game. Every new positive word we bring into our thoughts extends our experience and memory ability while bringing joy, peace, and happiness with it.

Write down all your favorite positive words:

_____

_____

_____

_____

_____

_____

_____

_____

_____

_____

_____

_____

_____

_____

_____

_____

_____

_____

_____

These are words Receive Joy has collected. We hope they inspire you to add to your own list above or add to ours.

BEAUTIFUL WORDS

abundant
accelerating
accomplished
accurate
achieving
acknowledgeable
active
admirable
admired
adorable
advanced
advantageous
adventure
adventurous
affection
affectionate
affirmations
affirmative
affluent
agreeable
aligned
alive
alluring
already
altruistic
always
amazing
amen
amiable
amusing
angelic
appealing
appreciated
appreciation

artistic
astonishing
astounding
astute
attentive
attractive
auspicious
authentic
awake
awakening
aware
awe
awe-inspiring
awesome
beaming
beautiful
beauty
bedazzling
believe
beneficial
benefit
best
better all the time
beyond
bless
blessed
blessings
bliss
blissful
blooming
bold
bountiful
brave
breath-giving

bright
brilliant
buoyant
calm
capable
caring
celebrate
celestial
centered
certain
change
charismatic
charming
cheerful
cherished
child-like
choice
clarity
classy
clear
clever
closeness
colorful
comfortable
commitment
communion
companionship
compassion
compassionate
compelling
competent
complete
confident
congratulations

BEAUTIFUL WORDS

connected

conscious

considerate

content

courageous

courteous

courtesy

creative

curious

cute

dancing

daring

dazzling

declare

deep

delicate

delicious

delightful

depth

desirable

determined

devoted

diligent

discerning

distinguished

divine

divine love

dominate

dream

dynamic

eagerness

easy

ecstatic

effective

efficient

elated

elegant

elite

eloquent

emotion

emotional

empowering

empowerment

encouraging

energetic

energizing

energy

engaging

engrossing

enigmatic

enjoyable

enjoyment

enriching

entertaining

enthralling

enthusiasm

enticing

epic

essential

established

eternal

eternity

ethereal

everlasting

evolving

exalted

excellent

exceptional

exciting

exemplary

exhale

exhilarating

experienced

exquisite

exuberant

eye-opening

fabulous

fair

faith

faithful

family love

famous

fancy

fantastic

fascinating

favorable

favored

fetching

fine

finish

first-class

first-rate

flattering

flourishing

flowing

focused

forevermore

forgive

fortunate

forward

free

freedom

BEAUTIFUL WORDS

friendly	ground-breaking	industrious
fruitful	growing	ingenious
fulfilled	growth	innocence
fulfilling	handsome	innovative
fun	happiness	insightful
generous	happy	inspiration
genius	harmonious	inspiring
gentle	harmony	instantaneously
genuine	headline-worthy	intelligent
gift	healed	interesting
gifted	healthy	intimacy
give thanks	heart	intuitive
gleaming	heartwarming	inventive
glee	heaven	invigorate
glittering	heavenly	inviting
glorifying	helpful	Jesus
glorious	honest	joyous
glory	honesty	jubilant
glowing	honorable	keen
goals	honored	kindhearted
golden	hope	kindness
good	hopeful	knowing
good-looking	hug	laudable
goodness	humorous	laugh
gorgeous	I am	lead
grace	iconic	legendary
graceful	ideal	let us
gracious	imaginative	life-giving
grand	imagine	light
gratifying	important	lightness
gratitude	impressive	likable
great	in tune	lively
greatness	increase	love
gripping	incredible	lovely

BEAUTIFUL WORDS

loving	one	prime
lucrative	open	proactive
luminous	optimism	prodigious
luscious	optimistic	productive
magical	outstanding	profitable
magnanimous	passionate	profound
magnetic	patience	progress
magnificent	peace	prominent
majestic	peaceful	prompt
marvelous	perfect	propitious
masterful	persevering	prosperous
meaningful	persistent	proud
mercy	phenomenal	pure
merit	pioneering	purify
meritorious	pitch-perfect	purpose-giving
mesmerizing	pivotal	quality
mighty	playful	quick
mind-changing	pleasant	quiet
mindful	pleasing	quintessential
miraculous	pleasure	radiance
monumental	plentiful	radiant
more	popular	rapturous
motivated	positive	rare
music	possible	ravishing
natural	power	ready
neat	powerful	real
new	prayer	receive
nice	precious	rediscover
noble	preeminent	refined
notable	prefer	refreshing
nourishing	preferable	regard
now	prepared	reimagine
nurturing	presence	rejoice
nutritious	pretty	rejuvenate

BEAUTIFUL WORDS

relationship	simple	terrific
relaxing	skillful	thankful
reliable	smart	thought-provoking
remarkable	smile	thriving
renewal	smooth	top-notch
renewing	solid	touching
reputable	soulful	trailblazing
resolute	sparkling	transcendent
resonance	special	transform
resourceful	spirit	transformational
respectful	spiritual	tremendous
resplendent	splendid	triumphant
restored	spontaneity	true
reverence	startling	trust
rewarding	stellar	trusting
rich	sterling	truth
right	stirring	truthful
righteous	strength	understanding
riveting	striking	unification
satisfied	strong	unique
satisfying	stunning	uplifting
self-control	sublime	useful
self-love	successful	valuable
self-reliant	suitable	versatile
sensational	sunny	vibrant
sensible	super	vibrations
sensitive	superb	victorious
sensual	supporting	vital
serene	supreme	vivacious
serenity	surprising	warm
shalom	talented	water
sharing	tantalizing	wealthy
sharp	tasteful	welcome
significant	tempting	well

BEAUTIFUL WORDS

well chosen	wisdom	world-class
well done	wise	worthy
well known	wonderful	wow
well-being	wondrous	zeal
whole	words	zest
wholesome	world peace	

Now that you have such a wonderful list of beautiful, positive words, there is plenty for which you can use it:

♥ Use your beautiful words when you describe experiences

♥ Use your beautiful words in your daily correspondence: add them to emails and texts you send

♥ Meditate on these words and be open to the feelings they induce

♥ Read these words out loud to imprint them within yourself

♥ Write them on your water bottle or water pitcher to imprint your water

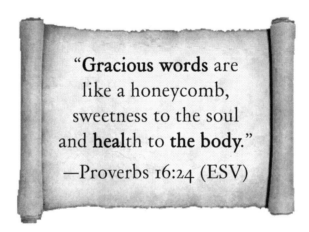

"**Gracious words** are like a honeycomb, sweetness to the soul and **health** to **the body**."
—Proverbs 16:24 (ESV)

Receive Joy created a recording of *Beautiful Words* to play in the car or whenever you use background music to increase your active vocabulary of positive words and to bless you and your environment. The frequencies of these words clear the air, soothe our pets, and imprint water (in our body, plants, pets, bottles, and pipes). Please refer to the back pages or www.receivejoy.com/shop for further information about all of Receive Joy's empowering products and how to acquire them.

"The **soothing tongue**
is a tree of life, but
a perverse tongue
crushes the spirit."

—Proverbs 15:4 (NIV)

TREE OF LIFE

54

Let us continuously read and write **positive inspirations and affirmations**. Positive messages fill our heart, mind, and subconscious with goodness and gladness. Anything we do repetitively anchors in our mind and becomes part of our habitual patterning. Anchoring helps to form new neural pathways. Affirming with words and actions at the same time is the most powerful anchoring. When we speak our affirmations while being physically active—for example as we are walking, jogging, jumping on a rebounder, or tapping—they are anchored even deeper.

Let us use physical anchoring to strengthen our affirmations. Be aware of every word in your affirmations. Every word counts. Please make sure they are entirely positive and beautiful. To help you receive inspiration, Receive Joy created an audio recording of positive affirmations called *Receive Inspiration*.

Here are examples of positive, beautiful affirmations:

- ♥ I expand my mind with beautiful words
- ♥ I speak positive words that bless myself and others
- ♥ I am privileged with constant awareness
- ♥ I live each day as the best day of my life
- ♥ I receive inspiration, new ideas, well-being, and beauty
- ♥ I am beautiful inside and out
- ♥ I love myself
- ♥ I am awesome
- ♥ God has blessed me
- ♥ I am worthy of God's love
- ♥ I am a true blessing to this world
- ♥ My life is light and easy

Please email us at ask@receivejoy.com and we will happily send you a multipage document of all positive inspirations. Let these beautiful, positive messages enhance your inner and outer dialog. Be gracious to yourself and others.

Speak these uplifting inspirations to yourself in front of the mirror. Record your own affirmations or use Receive Joy's 33-minute *Receive Inspiration* recording and listen to them while you attend to other tasks or during your meditation. In doing so, they will quickly be anchored into your subconscious and enhance your existing self-talk.

Write your ten most desired affirmations and repeat them out loud in front of your mirror twice a day.

1. _____
2. _____
3. _____
4. _____
5. _____
6. _____
7. _____
8. _____
9. _____
10. _____

God inspired men to write *The Holy Bible*, a book full of powerful declarations. *The Bible* shares with us the Power of God's Word. The Power of God's Word spoken forth activates and brings it to life. **Read *Bible* verses out loud** daily to call forth the glory of God.

We also call our *Bible* The Living Word, and every time it is read, recited, and preached, we breathe life into it, and people are blessed. Now is the time for us to tap into the positive ability of our mind and command our mind to align with the positivity God placed in our heart. Then, go forth in confidence **thinking great thoughts** and **speaking great words** of creation, love, encouragement, and abundance.

Positive thoughts become positive words to us as well as to others. Positive messages fill our hearts with goodness, gladness, and joy. What you say often becomes your predominant belief system and thus your reality. The words you speak have power over more than your own life. Our words are absorbed by our subconscious minds and the minds of the people around us. This allows us the **opportunity to be a blessing in our own lives and the lives of all beings**. Read the following prayer out loud:

Wonderous Creator of all that is,
You have created me with the ability to communicate my thoughts with my words. It is my choice to speak with clarity and love. It is this gift that allows me to verbalize my desires and feelings. May every thought I think and every word I speak be positive, encouraging, and loving. May all humanity be blessed by Your light shining through me and the words I use. Thank You, God. Amen.

"Let no corrupting talk come out of **your mouths**, but only such as is **good** for building up, as fits the occasion, that it may **give grace to those who hear.**"

—Ephesians 4:29 (ESV)

Chapter 7

ASK AND YOU SHALL RECEIVE

You can and will receive whatever you ask for. These are true words. All the words coming out of your mouth will influence your present and your future. When you **become aware of** your thoughts and **your words** and **believe** that everything you say creates the world around you, you begin to walk by faith. When you speak and live by steadfast faith, mountains will move in your world. Trust the total perfection right now. God has already given you everything. The power of God is voice activated. You have to **speak forth in faith what you desire**. Accept that you are highly favored and already blessed. You were chosen from the beginning! Trust the total perfection right now. God has supply for our every demand.

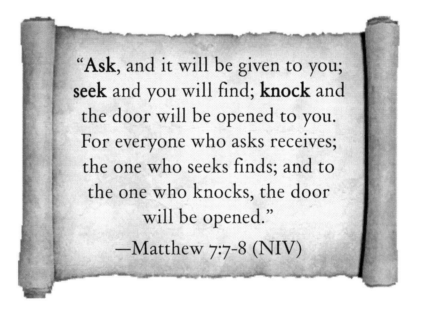

"**Ask**, and it will be given to you; **seek** and you will find; **knock** and the door will be opened to you. For everyone who asks receives; the one who seeks finds; and to the one who knocks, the door will be opened."

—Matthew 7:7-8 (NIV)

We have our complete inheritance as joint heirs with Jesus in the spiritual realm legally, and we come to possess this inheritance in the physical realm by speaking our divine birthright into being. Our complete inheritance was paid for and obtained 2,000 years ago on the cross, and we only receive it when we **accept** it as complete and **declare** it using good words of praise and thanksgiving. When we understand this, we can (possibly for the first time) experience a great revelation: **Our words are our keys to the Kingdom.**

Here is a beautiful story from my niece, who asked in declaration for her college experience exactly as she desired it and more:

"As I required help paying for college, the question was, What was I able to do about it? Going away to college and earning a four-year degree was important to me, so I did the first two things I thought of: pray and declare.

"I kept my grades up and visited my college advisor several times a week, collecting information about colleges and other organizations and the scholarships they offered. I required a full-ride scholarship to make my dream of attending university a reality.

"Through research and information, I found out that the number of full-ride scholarships was becoming rarer. It was a tall order to have college completely paid for through scholarships and grants. The summer before my senior year, I sat down with my family and **we prayed and declared** that I will receive a full-ride scholarship and more to the college that was right for me. Senior year began and I kept faith that God had a plan and applied for many colleges and scholarships.

"The advisor told me about two scholarships in particular. One was from a private organization offering $8,000 a year. I was chosen as the single nominee from my school to be considered for this private scholarship. The other was an invitation-only scholarship for housing or tuition at California State University Long Beach. Thus, I decided to apply there. I received both scholarships. The combination of the two scholarships and other grants amounted to more than enough to pay for all four years with extra money left for textbooks and school supplies.

"God's plan is always perfect. This experience confirmed that God has a plan and His Universe will order things for our benefit and His glory. Numerous things lined up that were beyond my asking. Many people have congratulated me for earning these scholarships. However, I know that the credit goes to God and the miracles that He performs daily.

"When I arrived at campus for my first week of classes, I immediately noticed the fleet of yellow shuttle buses driving around. I laughed when I saw the phrase 'I DECLARE' printed in large letters on the side of every bus! Throughout my time at the university, it continued to serve as a wonderful daily reminder of Step Two in Receive Joy's Nine Step Method presented in their book *Ask And You Shall Receive*. Thank you!"

God's powerful Universe is full of such an abundance of resources that it is beyond our minds' comprehension. Let us **keep asking and declaring with our tongue.**

Seek ye first the kingdom of the wonderous, and all things shall be added to you (Matthew 6:33.) This is a state of awareness. To enter this Kingdom, we shall **be as a child** (Matthew 18:3) living in a continuous state of joy and wonder. Let us look in wonder at all that is before us. Be awake to God's good everywhere. This life is wonderful.

Call forth good and vibrate with it. Feel good all the time. Call in your life by design and accept every desire and prayer as already done. Give thanks, be satisfied, and trust that you possess it. We call this act "asking."

Image. Image. Image. **Imagine and visualize** your life by design in your mind and then **speak the words** that describe it and call it in even before you see it manifested. **Add details** and **define why** you desire for something to transpire. Knowing why we desire something creates emotional connection to the outcome and aligns your head with your heart. Feel wonderful about asking, declaring, and calling in your greatness. Be happy and excited to receive your new being and creation.

Make sure your asking calls everything out in the present. **Speak and write in the present tense.**

Whenever we wish to create anything, let us write it down, as written words are easier to edit. Make a priority of **journaling**. Let us write down our words to bring them into this physical dimension and give form to our creation. There is great power in the pen.

Read over your words and **edit yourself three times**:

- ♥ Are all my words positive and uplifting?

- ♥ Do I speak and write in the present tense, as it has already happened and is here now?

- ♥ Do I say what I really wish to transpire? Is this what I really mean to say? Is this message as clear as it can be? Can I say it in fewer words?

- ♥ Why do I wish for these things to transpire?

- ♥ Have I praised God and given thanks in advance for receiving my desired outcome?

Speak aloud your positive askings in front of a mirror each morning and night. Visualize yourself with your manifested goals. The more imagining your imagination allows you, the faster and more accurate your asking will be.

Let us make a commitment to ourselves to speak words of success, abundance, prosperity, joy, kindness, and love.

God set up a powerful mechanism in the Universe that honors and carries out the agreement between two or more parties:

"Again I say to you, if **two** of you **agree** on earth about anything they ask, it will be done for them by my Father in heaven. For where two or three gather in my name, there am I with them."

—Matthew 18:19-20 (NIV)

We have this ability to create with the agreeing force of another individual. The other person can participate in agreement and encouragement of our set goals even when the other person is only slightly aware of the content. We can "high five" each other or have the other person initial our written statement, speak about it, or partake in whatever method with which we feel comfortable. Let us find a friend that is our second energy, our prayer partner, and our accountability partner to lift our spirit and vibration. Let us use the **Power of Agreement**.

".... In the mouth of **two or three witnesses** shall every word be established."

– II Cor 13:1 (KJV)

One of my brother's askings is to be a treasure finder, and I really love the idea of being a treasure finder myself. I wrote in my Daily Asking Journal that I will find treasures, gold, silver, and jewels. So far, I usually find treasures in thrift stores, so I am continually on the lookout. I said, "I am open for everything, God. You can bring me treasures all the time." The next morning, my mother and I went for a walk on the beach. I played around with my feet in the shallow water, when suddenly something was dancing around my toes.

Earlier that morning I was admiring an orange inchworm on a beautiful orange flower in my kitchen window, and thanked God for all the beautiful creatures He created; all in a very unique and fun way. As the thing by my feet was dancing the same way the inchworm moved, I thought it to be another animal. Looking closer, I picked it up and it turned out to be a shiny emerald bracelet. I found my first treasure!

Here are some other examples of Miracle Stories to inspire you to start **asking bigger** and **let God wow you with the how** it comes about:

When a couple visited our Miracle Group meetings for the first time, they learned that there is a way to petition God in prayer. Instead of begging, we **thank God for everything first**. He hears us and has already answered our "askings." We simply declare in positive words exactly what our heart desires including all parameters. We then **align ourselves with the matching vibration of satisfaction and receiving**, believing that we have already received it. Everything I require is already mine from the beginning of time. To bring it into the physical realm, we have to ask. Ask and you shall receive (Matthew 7:7–8.) Here is the Miracle Story that transpired within three weeks of them joining the meeting—manifesting their current dream of opening a bakery in town, as told by the owner: "This is *unbelievable*... well, it is actually believable. The magic of believing! After years, I met a friend again and she invited me to a meeting. We met at this amazing friend's house. While there, I was taught how to ask to receive. This was a Receive Joy Miracle Group meeting. People may say, 'I know how to ask.' Yet in this meeting, I learned a new way to ask.

"While I was there I was also reminded to use positive words and that I already have everything. In order to **attract what is already mine**, I simply have to believe that it is mine. I just needed to bring it into this physical world. I met with Receive Joy the same week so that I was able to learn a bit more since I was really intrigued. I wished for this bakery, and I stated that I was *trying* my best, I'm so good at this. Why is this *not* happening? I was coached on how to receive, 'You have to **allow it**. You have to **speak the word** and see it like it is already yours, like it is already here. Instead of pushing, just surrender to it.' Two days later, I received a call from a lady asking to have dinner with me. She asked me a lot of questions and I instantly knew her intent.

"She said, 'What are you doing now? I heard you two are really good. The word in town is that you are amazing bakers. How quick can you put a bakery together?' Considering everything I answered, 'Two months.' Her response: 'I am looking for two weeks.'

I almost declined and then something inside of me said, 'Just go with the flow. Surrender and see what happens.' I looked confidently at her and said, 'You know what? If anybody can do this it is definitely us.' Two weeks later everything was in place and we had this perfect, beautiful bakery. We also have amazing daily customers we know by name. It is truly amazing! And on top of it all, the bakery looks exactly like I imagined it, with all the parameters I wrote down when I asked in detail with Receive Joy. I envisioned it to look like my favorite French bakery in New York City, that makes me feel like being on the French Riviera.

"For me the pivoting point was to stop pushing and forcing. I just allowed this to come to be. Instead of me *trying* to control it, I allowed God to show up in amazing ways. Just **ask in detail using positive words and allow it to happen**."

After Hurricane Irma, many screened pool enclosures were blown out, including ours. The availability of screen in our town was diminished, to a point that even the screen repair companies were waiting for material. Although my friend owns a screen company, we were 25th out of over 400 on his list.

After a few weeks of waiting, my husband reminded me that we were hosting a dinner party at our house and he planned to grill outside. The mosquitoes, however, were plentiful. We had a second screen company come to the house that Monday to give us an estimate. I asked the guys where they normally purchase screen, and they told me the name of a hardware store in town. After inquiring, they also told me that the screen shipments come in on Tuesdays and Fridays. I replied, "Wonderful! Tomorrow is Tuesday and also my birthday, so I'll ask God to give me screen for my birthday." They laughed and said, "Good *luck*, lady!" I petitioned God and promised, "God, when You have this gift for me by Friday, I will be on my knees in praise and thanksgiving."

First thing the next day, I went to the hardware store and walked directly to the screen counter. They told me that they were out of screen and zero screen was expected. I found a lady who called to check for inventory at two other stores with the same result. However, she was kind enough to write up a purchase order for two rolls of 96-inch screen, because it was my birthday. She told me that when any screen comes in, she will have it delivered to this store. She also said that when they receive a delivery, she will call me and I can pay with my credit card over the phone. Before I left the store, I asked for the phone number of the manufacturer, and on my way home, I called the company to stay in my dream and grow my excitement about screen. The phone attendant explained to me the production procedure and how they had already increased to triple shifts and were delivering equally throughout the state, because everyone was asking for screen. They assured me, they were doing everything possible to supply the demand.

Early Friday morning, the hardware store called referencing an order and asking for my credit card number. At first, I was wondering what this was about, then all at once I remembered my birthday order! I paid and sent my daughter to the store. When she returned from the store, she had a fun story to tell: "When I went in the store and asked for my mom's screen, they looked at me as if I was out of this world and started laughing. However, my mom only sends me on errands with a reason, so I kindly asked them to look for the two rolls of screen I was to pick up with my mom's name on them. Just to humor me, they went to check. To their amazement, they came back with two rolls of screen with her name on it, and it was marked 'paid.' They were wondering how it got there. Was there a delivery? It was the weirdest look I saw on their faces."

When I asked my friend when he had time to install my screen, his first reaction was, "Which hardware store did you buy it at? I wish to buy screen for all my clients." I told him the name of the store and he called me back a few hours later to tell me, "I am at the store and they said that they are completely out of screen, and the last delivery they had was weeks ago! They denied ever having screen these past few days. How did you obtain the screen?" My reply was, "I know the owner." **God owns it all!** I went on my knees in praise and thanksgiving, happily driving my screen around in victory with a big smile on my face, thanking God profoundly every time I looked at it.

Since my friend was busy with other clients, I declared, "It is time to put up the screen on my lanai's cage." The second part of the order was the installation. I was also reminded that next time my asking can be more efficient by ordering the whole package at once: in this case, the screen plus the installation of it! I drove by the front gate of my community and asked for one of the men I knew working there to come by the house and install my screen. He came to the house the next morning, and in 24 hours, everything was done.

By God's grace I was able to visit every port as a passenger on an Asian cruise having applied for zero visas beforehand.

Working as a tour guide on cruise ships for many years, the cruise company and crew purser always made sure we had the right documentation and visas to go ashore. Having a German passport opens up the entry to many countries I visited, so it completely slipped my mind to look into the visa requirements when I was to join the vice captain of an American cruise line as a guest for a 40-day leg on an Asian cruise. I remember that we were always instructed that passengers can only go ashore in selective ports with a visa, and many people have to obtain their visa at a Chinese embassy before visiting China.

Shortly after boarding, the first purser asked me for my passport and visas. The only thing I thought of at this moment was to fall to my knees and pray, "God, you own the whole world. Please help me visit every country on this trip. I really wish to see everything, especially the Great Wall of China." At that moment I placed it on His altar. I appealed to the very power of His Universe, gave Him my desire and **why I desired it**. I knew **He can and will WOW me** with how he will do this because of His great love for me. The purser figured out the requirements necessary for German citizens to procure the visas, and the next day I found an envelope with plenty of paperwork for me to sign to apply for several visas to visit all the countries. I happily paid all the visa fees as this process was made so light and easy for me. Then I was informed that China just recently passed a new easy policy that allows German citizens to transit in China for 72 consecutive hours. Fabulous! The purser asked me whether I wished to go ashore in Xiamen for day one and Shanghai for days two and three or choose a three-day stay in Beijing. I told her I chose Beijing to see the Great Wall. Back in my cabin, I went on my knees again: "God, thank you so much for allowing me to see every country. I know you will make it happen. I know your love for me is beyond my comprehension and I am so glad that You are in my life. Again, what I really desire is to visit every city on the itinerary to see all of the world's beauty."

While I enjoyed many days and many different cities in Asia, I still had the desire to see all three Chinese ports: Xiamen, Shanghai, and Beijing. Before we reached China, miraculously the ship's itinerary was changed: The day at sea, after Shanghai, will be used for the ship and its passengers to clear in and out of South Korea. This created an additional 72 hours with a second transit visa in China. This miraculous stop made it possible for me to be ashore in all three Chinese ports. **With God, everything is possible!**

"And it shall come to pass, that **before they call, I will answer; and while they are yet speaking, I will hear.**"
—Isaiah 65:24 (KJV)

Please remember, God made the continual supply before your desire existed. In all things, we are already more than conquerors through Him who loves us.

"Yet in all these things
we are more than
conquerors through Him
who loved us".
—Romans 8:37 (NKJV)

All is well all the time. With God all things are possible. He is your constant supply. Use the greatness of His power. **When you guide your mind to think good thoughts, your mouth will share these good thoughts in the form of good words, and your deeds will follow in goodness.** You are complete. When you align your words to your awareness, when you state your intentions in truth-filled words, then **your faith in God's promises to men can be as small as a mustard seed**. With your words you activate the frequencies that form the matter around you. Changing your mind and beliefs to better-serving ones, along with optimizing your words, will correct and/or enhance the vibrations you emit to the Universe. Your words create your wonder, your belief, and your experiences. The Universe has a perfect language, and when you speak this language you have beautiful communication power. Learn to speak the language of God and His Universe. Remember the old, true saying: "A man is as good as his word." Let us live this reminder forevermore. God is so smart making the word final. As of today, come out of "babble-on" (Babylon) and step into your Promised Land. Transform your vocabulary, transform your life, and live by design.

Bless with your tongue. Speak life!

With Love and Gratitude,

Receive Joy

Thank you for reading *Blessed By The Tongue*. Here is one more exercise to complete for you to receive the maximum benefit from this book. Answer the following question and mail it back to us. Remember, the power is in the pen. You may also scan and email this page to ask@receivejoy.com

Receive Joy
1740 Persimmon Drive
Naples, FL 34109

What is your pearl of wisdom from this book?

_____

_____

_____

_____

_____

_____

_____

_____

_____

_____

_____

_____

_____

_____

_____

I will let go of the following phrase and/or belief on God's altar and replace it with:

_____

_____

_____

_____

_____

_____

Please pray for me and second my following asking:

_____

_____

_____

_____

_____

_____

Name: _____

Adress: _____

(Mobile) Phone: _____

Email: _____

❏ Yes, please add me to your prayer and newsletter list for updates on Receive Joy and invitations to Receive Joy's free Miracle Group.

TRANSFORMATIONAL VOCABULARY: PHRASES

ADVANCED AWARENESS	CREATIVE CHOICE
A deal you can't refuse	A deal you will absolutely wish to accept
A house divided can't stand	Together we stand
A method behind the madness	Using strategy
A price to pay	Consequences
A quitter never wins	Persevere
A woman's work is never done	A woman's work blesses everyone
A world filled with fear	View your world friendly
Absolutely unreal	Absolutely amazing; magical
Always too much to do	Ongoing variety
An awful lot	An abundance of
An infinite number of	An abundance of
Apparent obstacles	Illusions
Are you kidding me	Really; is it so
Aren't you wonderful	You are wonderful
Army of love	Oneness
As good as it gets	This is perfect; I am satisfied with this
Ask me no questions and I'll tell you no lies	Speak the truth
At last	Finally; yes; I'm so pleased/happy
At least; at the very least	It makes me happy when _____
Attached to nothing	Free
Bad attitude	Improve your attitude
Bad idea	Let's come up with a better idea
Bad luck	A super challenge; open to a better fortune
Bad news	Be aware; different expectation
Be real	Think through it; stay grounded

ADVANCED AWARENESS	CREATIVE CHOICE
Beat it	Go forth; succeed; please leave
Beating myself up	Hard on myself
Beating the odds	Winning
Believe in the impossible	Exercise faith
Believe it or not	You'll be pleased to know _____
Benefit of the doubt	Trust
Better luck next time	The best is yet to come; stay with it
Better safe than sorry	Be careful; be prepared
Beyond a doubt	For sure
Beyond the shadow of a doubt	Certainly
Bite the bullet	Take action; just do it
Blast from the past	Fun memory; I recognize that
Blood, sweat and tears	Lots of energy
Bloody hell	Oh wow
Bouncing off the walls	So much energy
Boundless energy	Full of energy
Boundless possibilities	Many possibilities
Boxed in	Desiring freedom
Break a leg	I wish you success; enjoy the show
Break all the chains	Be free; enjoy your freedom
Break the silence	Speak up
Broken world	Currently
Bullshit your way	Succeed by all means
Burden is lifted	Light and easy
Burn in hell	Leave me be
Business is poor	I am ready for a miracle

ADVANCED AWARENESS	CREATIVE CHOICE
By default	By design
By hook or crook	By all possibilities
Can I be honest with you	Honestly, _____
Can never be depleted	Always full of resources
Can not	Consider _____
Can you doubt even for a moment	Stay in faith always
Can't afford it	I really wish to have _____
Can't be interfered with	Let it be
Can't be moved	Fixed in place
Can't be tampered with	Is secure
Can't be too careful	Be prepared
Can't get any better	This is perfection
Can't have	Shall have
Can't help but _____	I am [say what you really mean] _____
Can't refuse	Absolutely agree to
Can't resist	Very appealing
Casting the burden	Freeing oneself
Chances are	I think
Change is tough	Change becomes easier
Change takes time and effort	Decide now
Chasing your tail	Stay focused on your goals
Cheaters never prosper/win	Be honest
Childhood is your happiest time	Your entire life is full of opportunities to rejoice
Come to your senses	Wake up
Compromised immune system	Activated immune system
Conspiracy (theory)	Other's opinions

ADVANCED AWARENESS	CREATIVE CHOICE
Could not agree more	I absolutely agree; we are in 100% agreement
Cut me some slack	Have compassion
Cut you/someone off	Stop
Damn it	Oops
Dead last	Last place
Dead loser	Room for improvement
Dead on	Spot on
Dead serious	Assuredly
Dead wrong	Missing the point
Debbie Downer	Choose positive thoughts and words
Debt free	Financially sound; everything is paid in full
Deep despair	Greatly questioning
Despite what you think	This is the truth
Didn't miss anything	Captured everything
Didn't want that	I prefer _____
Do no harm	Help
Do not abstain	Keep going; partake
Do or die	Just do it
Do the fearless thing	Do the courageous thing
Do you mind	Will you please
Does not explain	It just is
Doing nothing	Relaxing; simply being
Don't analyze	Listen to your inner self
Don't ask me why	God knows
Don't be _____	Be _____

ADVANCED AWARENESS	CREATIVE CHOICE
Don't be anxious	Be calm; relax
Don't be ashamed	Stand strong; live your perfection
Don't be concerned about what they say	Your business is your own
Don't be confused	Stay clear; stay focused
Don't be so hard on yourself	Love yourself
Don't be so negative	Be more positive
Don't be such a chicken	Please go forth with confidence
Don't be too concerned	Let it go; stay calm
Don't beat around the bush	I prefer you to be direct
Don't beat yourself up	Love yourself; own your life
Don't believe the lies	Believe the truth; seek the truth
Don't blame conditions	It's all you and the choices you make
Don't bother	All is well; let it be; I am fine
Don't bother me	Let me be
Don't break it	Leave it whole
Don't bring me down	I choose joy
Don't call	Trust; allow peace
Don't chicken out	Stay the course
Don't concern yourself with	This is for me to think about
Don't cry	Be at peace
Don't despair	Be of good cheer; keep your faith
Don't despise	Have compassion
Don't disturb	Let it be
Don't do it	Do _____
Don't do it again	Stop it
Don't do this	Rather do this

73

ADVANCED AWARENESS	CREATIVE CHOICE
Don't doubt	Have faith
Don't drift	Stay focused
Don't eat it	Save it; leave it be
Don't even think about it	Drop it; stop it
Don't ever make the (same) mistake	Be certain; be prepared
Don't expect _____	Expect _____
Don't expect sympathy	Get over yourself
Don't fail	Succeed
Don't fall	Walk steady
Don't fear	Have faith; love
Don't feed them to the wolves	Have some compassion
Don't feel bad about _____	Feel good about _____
Don't follow	Lead
Don't fool around	Stay focused
Don't force it	Let it happen; accept it; let it flow gently
Don't forget	Remember
Don't fuel the fire	Be part of the solution; be constructive
Don't get hung up on	Move on
Don't get me wrong	What I am really saying here is _____
Don't get stuck	Continue on; keep on moving
Don't give in	Remain steadfast
Don't harm	Keep them well
Don't hesitate	Go/flow with it; take immediate action
Don't hold a grudge	Forgive
Don't hold back	Use your full potential; take action
Don't judge	Be in acceptance; have compassion

ADVANCED AWARENESS	CREATIVE CHOICE
Don't judge by appearance	Accept all appearances
Don't judge yourself	Accept and love; love yourself
Don't leave	Please stay
Don't leave me behind	Help me stay with you
Don't let	Allow only
Don't let anything stop you	Keep on; stay the course
Don't let me _____	I will _____
Don't let me fall	Hold me up
Don't let me hate	Let me love
Don't let me miss it	Help me see it; remind me
Don't let other people _____	It is all me
Don't let the dream fade	Keep your dreams alive
Don't let us down	We super believe in you; you can do it
Don't lie	Tell the truth
Don't limit	Allow
Don't limit God	Allow all possibilities
Don't limit yourself	Use your full potential; express yourself
Don't listen to them	Stay your course; listen to your own heart
Don't live in fear	Live in faith
Don't look back	Stay focused on the target
Don't lose your way	Stay on track; stay focused
Don't make a sound	Be quiet
Don't make excuses	Just do it
Don't make me hate _____	Let me love _____
Don't make the mistake of _____	Be certain; use caution

ADVANCED AWARENESS	CREATIVE CHOICE
Don't mess up	Do a good job
Don't miss out	Participate; come join in
Don't miss your chance	This is your opportunity
Don't overthink it	Move on
Don't panic	Stay calm
Don't pay full price	Receive a discount
Don't poke your eye out	Be safe
Don't procrastinate	Motivate yourself; just do it; take action now
Don't put limits on yourself	Be open to receive everything you dream of
Don't remove	Keep it there
Don't repeat it	Do _____ instead; keep this to yourself
Don't settle for less	Go for more; be certain
Don't speak	Remain silent
Don't stab me in the back	Be upfront with me
Don't stand in the way	Move over; stand clear
Don't stay boxed in	Expand; open up to new possibilities
Don't stop me	Allow me to carry on
Don't stress about _____	Be comfortable with _____
Don't stumble and fall	Walk steady
Don't suffer	Stay well
Don't sweat the details	Focus on the target
Don't sweat the small stuff	See the bigger picture
Don't talk	Remain silent
Don't think about it	Stay focused
Don't think it is impossible	Believe

ADVANCED AWARENESS	CREATIVE CHOICE
Don't think, just do	Take action now; just do it
Don't throw them under the bus	Have some compassion
Don't touch	Leave it be
Don't use idol words	Use ideal words
Don't whine	Look on the bright side
Don't wig out	Remain calm
Don't worry	Be happy; be encouraged; take heart
Don't worry about it	Keep your faith
Don't worry about tomorrow	Be excited about today
Don't worry about what they say	Trust yourself
Don't you dare	How about you _____
Don't/Do not	Rather/I prefer/Please do _____
Doom and gloom	Look on the bright side
Double trouble	Lots of energy
Drifting aimlessly	Focus on your goals and take action
Driving me crazy/nuts	Please stop it
Drop-dead gorgeous	Extremely gorgeous
Easier said than done	This currently challenges me; I will rise to the occasion
Eating me up	Constantly on my mind
Effortless/Effortlessly	Easy
Endless examples	Many examples
Energy vampire	Too much
Even if it kills me	Anyways
Even if you don't	Look on the bright side
Expect the worst to happen	Prepare; call in a miracle
Extraordinary	Super; great

ADVANCED AWARENESS	CREATIVE CHOICE
Facing a challenge	Have a new opportunity
Fall into a routine	Build and follow a routine
Falling in love	Welcoming in love
False peace	Illusion
Fat and lazy	Ready for improvement
Fat chance	Dream big
Fear is impossible	Faith is everlasting
Fear of death	Acceptance of change
Fear of loss	Accept change
Fear/scare tactics	Motivation tactics
Fear-based marketing	Influential marketing
Fight against	Stand tall and move into your greatness
Fight for it	Be excited to have it
Fight the good fight	Stand strong
Fighting boredom	Creating excitement
Fighting chance	A possibility
Filthy rich	Beautifully rich; happily wealthy
Find a way	God is the way, the truth and the life
Fixed income	Ever increasing income
Follow the news	Use your common sense
For God's/Heaven's sake	For goodness sake; oh my goodness
For the life of me I can't see the point	What is the message
Forget about that	All is well
Forget that	Focus on the victory
Free of fear; fear-free	Absolute trust in God
Frightfully exciting	Very exciting

ADVANCED AWARENESS	CREATIVE CHOICE
From our failure comes _____	We learn from everything
Full of shit	Lacking honesty
Get ahead	Advance; prosper; become more
Get out of here	Please leave; oh really
Get real	Consider this
Getting worse	More challenging
Give me a break	I am ready for God's favor
Give me some slack	Have patience
Give myself a break	Allow myself some joy
Go to hell	Enough
God can't fail	God reigns victorious
God damn it	God bless all
God damn you	God bless us
God forbid	Even when _____
God is (already) there	God is here now
God only knows why	It is beyond me
Going downhill	Focus on God
Going out of my mind	So much variety
Going to get	Now have
Good luck	I super believe in you
Greatest fear	I feel in my heart that _____
Grow worse and worse	Facing more obstacles
Guard against	Set boundaries
Hammer it into your memory	Promise to remember
Hammered in	Imprinted
Hard times	Contrast

ADVANCED AWARENESS	CREATIVE CHOICE
Hard work and long hours bring riches	Faith alone in Christ alone (lest any man boast)
Hard work/Work hard	I gave that a lot of energy
Hard-earned dollars/savings	Income and savings
Hard-earned/Hard-fought	Well-earned; valuable
Hard-fought victories	Well-earned victories
Hate to miss it	I will be with you in spirit; I prefer to be there
Have no right to	I will make my own decisions
Have not; haven't	Have yet to
He has a Napoleon complex	He is very confident
He is a failure	I have yet to see his greatness
He's hammered	He's had enough
Health issue	Health status
Hellish thoughts	Opposing thoughts
Help you tackle	Help you succeed
Here is my problem	I wish to share with you
Hit me with your best shot	Ask me
Hit the ball out of the park	You excelled
Hit the road	Go forth in success
Holy cow	Wow
Holy crap	Wow
Holy mackerel	Wow
Holy shit	Wow
Hopefully there's no _____	I declare there will be _____
How bad can it be/get	The fact of the matter is _____
How bad can life be	How fun life can be

ADVANCED AWARENESS	CREATIVE CHOICE
How hard it is to break through	Just do it
I adore you more than life itself	I adore you
I ask not _____	I ask for _____
I can't accept it	I will soon align with it; I allow myself to accept
I can't afford it	I really wish to have _____
I can't affort to _____	My target is _____
I can't believe _____	Wow
I can't do it	I have other plans; God, please help
I can't explain it	I am compelled to; it is miraculous
I can't fail	I will be victorious
I can't get over it	God is a way maker
I can't go there	I wish to stay positive
I can't help but _____	I am compelled to _____
I can't help it	I am compelled to do it; I am learning discipline
I can't lose it	It will always be mine
I can't say that	I will say _____
I can't separate	It is one; unified; united
I can't stay	I will go now
I can't wait	It is so exciting; I am ready and able
I couldn't believe _____	It surprised me when _____
I couldn't get _____	I am yet to have _____
I didn't believe	That surprised me
I didn't dare	I chose to _____
I didn't do it	It's beyond me; I am innocent
I don't believe it	I shall believe

ADVANCED AWARENESS	CREATIVE CHOICE
I don't blame you	I agree
I don't care	I'll pass; it's someone else's blessing
I don't care if I lose	Every outcome is a good outcome
I don't doubt it	Absolutely; with certainty; for sure; I agree
I don't have time	I have the rest of my life
I don't know	I am yet to understand; it will come to me
I don't know what to do	I will call on God for guidance
I don't know which end is up	I will reorganize myself
I don't like _____	I prefer _____
I don't really care	You choose
I don't stand a chance	Thank you God, for being my divine supply and savior
I don't want it	I pass; I prefer _____
I don't want to _____	I prefer to; I rather; I am happier with _____
I don't want to quit	I will keep on
I don't want you to feel bad	I am considering your feelings
I doubt it	You may be right
I fear	I trust
I feel awful	I require rest; I repent
I feel awful for you	I have compassion for you
I feel bad for you	I have compassion for you; I understand
I feel terrible about _____	I feel compassion for _____
I got lost	I took a detour
I hate to leave	I choose to go

ADVANCED AWARENESS	CREATIVE CHOICE
I hate you	I feel _____
I have a closed mind	Open my mind God
I have a sinking feeling	Return to my strong vibration
I have been struggling	I have been experiencing contrast
I have made many mistakes	I've tried it many ways
I have never failed	I always succeed; I can do/accomplish everything I set my mind on
I have no idea	I am still seeking the answer
I have no job	I am in the process of creating my perfect career
I have no privacy	I now declare some privacy
I have no resentment toward him	I have compassion for him
I have no troubles	All is well
I have no work	I am ready to work
I have the jitters	I shall calm myself
I have to fight for it	It requires a lot of energy
I haven't got a chance	I will pray; God help
I just lost it	I shall remember where it is; I will be/remain calm
I know nothing about that	That is new to me
I love you to death	I love you dearly
I made the mistake of _____	I allowed _____
I need you desperately	I enjoy being with you
I never get a break	I work continuously
I never really learned that	That is above my current skill set
I refuse to _____	I choose to _____
I refuse to be interested in _____	I choose to be interested in _____

ADVANCED AWARENESS	CREATIVE CHOICE
I refuse to believe that _____	I choose to believe _____
I remember, I just forgot	I know this
I see the obstacles in my way	I focus on the target
I shall not want	God supplies everything
I want to hurt them	My emotions are spiraling
I want to quit	I require more motivation
I want to see her so badly	I am excited to see her
I was dying to work with you	I am excited to work with you
I wasn't aware	Thank you for bringing it to my attention
I will never forget	I will always remember
I will never go back	I am happy to be here now
I will not die	I will live
I will not lose	I always win
I wish I could	I am looking at possibilities; I desire to; I can _____
I won't forget that	I promise to remember that
I wouldn't complain	I am pleased/satisfied
I wouldn't miss it for the world	I am excited to attend
I'll be damned	I'll be blessed
I'm against it	I prefer something different; I am for God
I'm at war with	I am engaging in contrast
I'm bad at this	This is worth practicing
I'm confused	I desire clarity/understanding
I'm exhausted	I require rest
I'm fearless	I am full of faith
I'm feeling your pain	I understand

ADVANCED AWARENESS	CREATIVE CHOICE
I'm in a hurry	I have a lot to accomplish right now
I'm losing my mind/I lost my mind	I shall take a moment to center my thoughts
I'm miserable	I feel off
I'm not asleep	I am awake
I'm not going to lose you	You are always in my heart
I'm not good enough	I am worthy of God's love
I'm not losing my hair over it	It will work itself out
I'm not moving	I am staying right here
I'm not sure	I desire clarity
I'm sick of always/It's a pain to always	I prefer to _____; I rather _____
I'm sick of it	I have enough for now
I'm so broke	I welcome in abundance
I'm so broke I can't pay attention	Yet to call in God's continual supply of abundance
I'm so worried	I care about
I'm starving	I feel so hungry
I'm tired of being sick and tired	I welcome more energy, health, harmony and peace into my life
I'm trying to sleep	Please let me sleep
If it is not this, then it is something else	Life ebbs and flows; God is good
If worse comes to worse	In the event of _____
If you are not sure	When you desire more clarity
If you are not too successful	When you wish to aim for more success
If you can get to it	After you complete everything, then _____, please
If you don't let go	Please let go

ADVANCED AWARENESS	CREATIVE CHOICE
If you don't mind	Please, I appreciate it when you _____
If you don't remember anything else	Promise to remember this
If you have not already _____	Will you; can I ask a favor of you
If you want it bad enough	When you truly desire it
If you're not happy	I aim to please
Ignorance is bliss	Live in the moment
Ill effects	Consequences
Impossible situation	A situation beyond me; God help
In a battle with	Creating contrast with
In a hurry	Occupied
In an unexpected way	In a surprising way
In despair	Temporarily confused
In due time	Now
In God's timing	Now; miraculously
In the right time	Now
In the trenches	In the midst of it
In times of need	Asking for additional support
In your/their face	Direct
Inexhaustible energy	Continuous energy
Is there a problem	Is everything good
Is there something impairing you	Do you require further support
It breaks my heart	I really feel it
It can't be done	With God everything is possible
It can't go wrong	It will succeed
It can't last	It will run its course
It can't/couldn't hurt	Let's try; it helps

ADVANCED AWARENESS	CREATIVE CHOICE
It didn't happen	There is always another opportunity
It does not contain	It only contains _____
It doesn't matter	It's alright
It doesn't mean _____	It means _____
It doesn't need to be hard	It's simple
It kills me/It's killing me	I desire better; I am very emotional about it
It may not hurt	It will be fine; all is well
It never stops	It continues on
It pains me	I desire better
It shouldn't be this hard	It shall be easy
It takes hard work	It takes prayer and faith
It was awful	It was interesting
It wasn't me	Keep investigating
It will blow your mind	It will expand your mind
It will never be a success	Focus your energy and it will be a success
It will not be difficult	It is easy
It will probably never happen	There is always a possibility
It won't be easy	Diligence is required
It's a bad fit	I desire a better fit; it's someone else's blessing
It's a jungle out there	There is a lot of variety all around
It's a shame	I prefer; I wish
It's a war zone	Temporary chaos
It's a war zone in there	There is a lot happening in there
It's an absolute crime	I prefer it a different way
It's a bad fit	It's someone else's blessing

ADVANCED AWARENESS	CREATIVE CHOICE
It's difficult	It requires focus
It's easy to blame	Own it; it's all me
It's getting worse	It appears more challenging
It's going to get worse	I'll keep my eyes on God
It's hard to change	Change takes practice
It's my fault	I allowed
It's never too late	God is in the miracle business
It's no accident	It's by design
It's no secret	It's common knowledge
It's not a battle	Life is a game
It's not a game, it's real life	Please listen
It's not complicated	It's easy
It's not easy	I will create an easier way
It's not fool-proof	Be aware
It's not going well	It requires more prayer
It's not just	It just is
It's not my/your business	Mind your own business
It's not that bad	It is actually good
It's not worth losing sleep over	Keep it in perspective
It's not your fault	You allowed _____
It's really sad	I have compassion
It's scary	It's overly exciting
It's so hard	It's currently challenging
It's such a tragedy	I am experiencing _____
It's terrible	I have a better expectation
It's the least I can do	I am happy to help

ADVANCED AWARENESS	CREATIVE CHOICE
It's their fault	I allowed
It's to die for	It's wonderful
It's too much work	So much energy
It's what it is	All is well
Judge not	Accept and love
Just deal with it	Next; move on
Just for the hell of it	Just for the fun of it
Just missed it	Life progresses according to plan; next
Kill two birds with one stone	All at once
Killing time	Waiting
Knock yourself out	Go for it; do your best
Knowledge locked up in their bones	God's knowledge is everywhere
Knows no bounds	Open to all possibilities
Knows no defeat	Always succeeds
Laced with negativity	Ready for positivity
Lack and limitation	Abundance and freedom
Lack of _____	Currently creating _____
Lack of limitation	Wide open
Last but not least	One more thing; the last important item is _____
Lazy bastard	Be motivated
Learn to accept it	Count it all joy; create better
Leave your past behind	Focus on today
Less bumpy	Smooth
Less critical	More accepting
Less is more	Simplify
Less pain	Feel good/well

ADVANCED AWARENESS	CREATIVE CHOICE
Less stress	Calm; at peace
Let not your heart be troubled	Stay in good cheer
Let sleeping dogs lie	It's good enough
Let's get ready	Let's be ready
Life can be so hard	Life is full of variety
Life is a battle	Life is full of opportunity
Life is not easy	I choose to view my world friendly
Life is so hard	Life is currently challenging
Lifetime of misery	Allowed sadness
Like it or not	Like it and enjoy it
Limited in your ideas	Be open
Limited number available	Perfect supply
Limiting beliefs	Old agreements
Long suffering	Patient
Lose weight	My ideal weight is _____
Loss of memory	Living in the current moment; a keen memory
Lost cause	God help
Love knows no distance	Love prevails
Love without end	Eternal love; everlasting love
Make it happen	Allow God's grace
Make no mistake	My point is _____
Massive psychological shift	Better thoughts
Maybe you can	You can
Midlife crisis	New greatness; a new chapter in my life
Misery loves company	Like attracts like
Money doesn't grow on trees	God is our continual supply

ADVANCED AWARENESS	CREATIVE CHOICE
Monstrous success	Great success
More or less	Almost; pretty much
Most people are extras in their own movie	Be the lead in your life; author your desires
My bad	I am responsible; sorry
My phone is dead/dying	My phone has to be charged
My problem is _____	How can I solve _____
My worst nightmare	My greatest challenge; my deepest desire
Nearly every success is built on failure	Every situation is a gift and an opportunity
Needless to say	Obviously
Negativity has no part in my life	I only allow positivity in my life
Neither slumbers nor sleeps	Stays alert and awake
Never a dull moment	Always full of excitement
Never a question in my mind	Absolutely
Never argue	Always agree
Never be completed	Still open
Never been defeated	Always victorious
Never can be taken from me	Will always remain with me
Never cease	Prevail; keep on
Never ceases to amaze me	Always something new
Never ceasing	Continues on
Never come to a conclusion	Yet to decide
Never compromise	Remain steadfast; stick to the plan
Never conflict	Stay in agreement and flow
Never confused	Always clear
Never curse	Always bless

ADVANCED AWARENESS	CREATIVE CHOICE
Never died	Lives on
Never done before	New experience
Never doubting	Absolute certainty
Never enough	Always ready to receive more; room for more
Never ever	Absolutely
Never failed	Always succeeded
Never fails	Always happens; consistently
Never fall	Remain standing
Never forget	Always remember; promise to remember
Never fully	Partially
Never get over it	I choose to advance
Never give up	Stay the course
Never go back	This is your new standard
Never going to get there	On my way
Never hate	Always love
Never hinder	Always allow
Never late	Always punctual
Never leave	Stay
Never let go	Hold on
Never let me miss a trick	Always keep me focused
Never look back	Stay in the present moment
Never lose sight of	Always focus on
Never mind	All is well
Never misses a trick	Alert; always focused
Never return	Stay away
Never say never	Everything is possible

ADVANCED AWARENESS	CREATIVE CHOICE
Never sought-after	Secret; stay away
Never stop	Persevere
Never talk	Remain quiet
Never too late	Now
Nitty gritty	Final details
No attachment	Free
No boundaries	Wide open
No clue	Yet to know
No competition	The best
No confusion	Clarity; crystal clear
No control over	In God's hands
No doubt	Absolutely; of course; for sure; I agree
No effort	Light and easy
No emotional response	Just love
No going back	Onward always
No harm done	All is well
No intention of slowing down	I will keep on
No kidding	Really; seriously
No limit to what you can do	You are completely capable; wide open
No limits	Wide open
No longer	Choose to move on
No loss	All gain
No lost opportunities	Continuous opportunities; wide open
No matter what	By all means; for sure
No more	Stop
No more dummies	I welcome smart people

ADVANCED AWARENESS	CREATIVE CHOICE
No more pain	Feel good
No more stress	Calm; at peace
No mysteries	Only absolutes
No negative impact	Safe; all is well
No nonsense	Straightforward
No obstacles	Wide open
No one can shut it	It remains open
No one else	Only you
No one gets to me	I believe in myself
No one is perfect	We are perfect as we are; God made us as we are
No one knows	God knows
No one knows what you are capable of	Live up to your capability
No one should have to suffer	Grace is for everyone
No pain	Feel great; perfect health; restored and renewed
No pain, no gain	Step up to the requirements
No power to hurt	Only power to bless
No problem	Blessings; my pleasure; you're welcome
No question	Absolutely
No questions asked	I trust you
No secrets	Open book
No such luck	Let's turn things our way
No such thing as chance	Everything is divinely inspired
No thrill	I prefer _____
No trouble at all	It is a pleasure
No two ways about it	The best way is _____

ADVANCED AWARENESS	CREATIVE CHOICE
No way	Wow; there is always a way
No wonder	Obviously; of course
No worries	Be happy; I'm happy to do this for you
Nobody can deny _____	It is true; everyone agrees with _____
Nonresistance/Nonresistant	Neutrality; surrender; flow
Not a bad idea	That's actually a good idea
Not a chance	With God all things are possible
Not a good place to be	Move on please
Not a problem	Blessings; it's a pleasure; you are welcome
Not/Never alone	God is with you
Not appreciated	Desire to be recognized
Not at all	You're welcome; my pleasure
Not bad	Good
Not bad at all	Looks good
Not be taken away	Will remain
Not by a long shot	Redirect your focus; try again
Not closed	Wide open
Not dead	Alive
Not doing enough	I can do more
Not expected	Surprise
Not forgotten	Remembered
Not going to lose	Keeping; hold on to
Not in your right mind	You might wish to rethink it
Not know it	Yet to understand it
Not lost	Found
Not moved	Steady; in place; remain the same

ADVANCED AWARENESS	CREATIVE CHOICE
Not only	Also; and
Not possible	With God all things are possible
Not really important	Focus on what is most important
Not return void	Accomplish its purpose
Not sought-after	Secret
Not terribly/that expensive	Affordable
Not the one	I prefer _____
Not to say	In addition
Not too happy about that	I prefer _____
Not too long ago	Recently
Not too shabby	Looks good
Not under law	Under grace
Not yet	Yet to be; soon
Nothing but	Only
Nothing can hold us back	Moving forward; we will succeed
Nothing can interfere with	There is a clear path
Nothing can separate	There is only oneness
Nothing can separate you from _____	Always connected to _____
Nothing can stop us	Whatever it takes; we will succeed
Nothing ever ends	It all continues on
Nothing I can't do	I can achieve everything
Nothing is lost	It is all here
Nothing less than	Only
Nothing negative	Only positivity
Nothing offends me	Everything brings me joy
Nothing other than	Only _____

ADVANCED AWARENESS	CREATIVE CHOICE
Nothing to be afraid of	All is good; all is well; there is only God's grace
Nothing to be sorry about	It is alright
Nothing to fear	All is good; all is well; there is only God's grace
Nothing to oppose	Only
Nothing to us	Comes easily
Nothing wrong	Everything is perfect
Nothing wrong with it	It is perfect; it is alright
Nothing wrong with you	You are great; you are healthy
Old habits die hard	Welcome in change
Old hag	Mature
Only thing to fear is fear itself	Have faith, everything else is an illusion
Our problem is not that we don't know	We know everything necessary to advance
Out of his mind	Unique
Out of luck	Imagine something better; turn things our way
Overt all the suffering and pain	Encourage and spread love
Packing on the pounds	Pay attention to your body
Painful separation	Emotionally intense
Path of least resistance	Light and easy way
Pissed off	Excited
Plan of attack	Victorious plan; detailed plan
Poor child	Blessed child
Price to pay	Consequences
Put fear into the heart of	Take action

ADVANCED AWARENESS	CREATIVE CHOICE
Raining cats and dogs	Heavy rain
Raised to believe	I am changing now
Rather be safe than sorry	Be prepared
Ready to check out	I am complete
Reduce pain and stress	Feel good
Regardless of	Anyway
Remove all doubt	Believe
Rough and tough	Strong
Running in circles	Stay focused on your goals
Same old	Once again; repeated; familiar
Save it for a rainy day	Use it now; we have all the resources we require
Scare the shit out of me	That's something
Scared me to death	Surprised me
Scared to death	I am feeling very emotional; testing my faith
Scary times	Lots of variety available for all
Screw you	Leave me be
Search the unknown	Search beyond; be creative
Second to none	You are the best
Seems a little reckless	Are you sure
Self-inflicted misery	My choice; I allowed _____
Shame on you	You can do better
She will kill me	Pray for me
Should not _____	I prefer _____
Shouldn't have any trouble	Shall be light and easy
Shoveling shit	An opportunity to share blessings

ADVANCED AWARENESS	CREATIVE CHOICE
Sick and tired	Ready to advance
Sleepless nights	Awake all night
Slow road to recovery	Healing is here now
Smashing success	Brilliant success
So bad	Remains interesting
Solving problems	Creating solutions; solution-oriented
Some may never get there	Everyone is where they are meant to be
Something is wrong	Something is off
Soul sucking	Too much
Speak of the devil	Oh, it is you; here they are now
Spiritual warfare	God has gone before me and won
Spontaneous remission	God's miracle; instant healing
Stay clear of trouble	Walk a straight upright path
Stick to my guns	Stay focused
Stop agonizing over	Move on
Stop criticizing	Be encouraging
Stop doomscrolling	Be productive
Stop self-sabotage	Take action
Stop shooting yourself in the foot	Move out of your own way
Stop smoking	Take care of your lungs
Stressed out	Enough
Struggling to make ends meet	Calling in my prosperity
Stumble on greatness	Call forth greatness
Stumbled upon	Divinely inspired
Suffer the consequences	Experience variety; actions create consequences

ADVANCED AWARENESS	CREATIVE CHOICE
Tackle it	Complete it
Take an honest look	Exercise compassion
Take away the pain	Feel good
Talk about anything but _____	Let's focus on _____
Target your trouble spots	Be aware
Terribly beautiful	Very beautiful
Terribly new	Very new
Terrific fear	Concerned
That can't be	Wow
That makes no sense	Using my common sense _____
That was a terrible experience	That was something
That was dumb	That was something
That's a hard bone to chew	That's serious
That's a scary thought	Let's have a better thought
That's illogical	My logic says _____
That's not a bad idea	That's a good idea
That's not for me	I prefer; that is for someone else
That's not for you	That is for someone else
That's not going to happen	There's always a chance; I will pass on it
That's not learning	Please learn
That's not my problem	I choose to focus on _____
That's not our problem	The temporary challenge is _____
That's not realistic	Dream on
That's not so dumb	That's genius
That's pathetic	That can use some improvement
That's so stupid	Next

ADVANCED AWARENESS	CREATIVE CHOICE
That's terrible	I have a better expectation
That's the problem	That is the gift
That's the worst thing you could do	There are many better options
That's the worst way	Every other solution is better
That's too bad	I understand
The battle is won	I am victorious
The blind leading the blind	Like attracts like
The crazy part is	The amazing part is
The depths of depression	Ready for joy
The devil made me do it	I chose to _____
The enemy	The opposite charge
The hell with it	I am done
The odds are against you	God is on your side
The only limit	Think beyond
The sky is the limit	Everything is possible; so many possibilities; vast as the sky
The struggle is real	With God, all things are possible; rejoice in Jesus
The tail is wagging the dog	You are the leader; start leading
The trouble with	My concern about
The unexpected happens	Surprise happens
The unknown factor	Change
The warrior within me	The David within me
The world is out to get me	I allowed _____
The worst is yet to come	Prepare
The worst part was	The most concerning part was
There are limits to what you can do	With God everything is possible

ADVANCED AWARENESS	CREATIVE CHOICE
There are no accidents	There are only choices we've made
There are no disappointments	There are only happy surprises
There are no limitations	Everything is possible
There are no obstacles	The way is free and clear; there is a clear path
There is no competition	Everything is here for you
There is no end/limit to it	There is a great amount of; it is continuous
There is no end/limit to what you can do	You can do all things with God
There is no getting around it	Take a direct path; face it
There is no place like home	There is a place like home
There is no power in evil	There is absolute power in good
There is no room for mistakes	Please be precise
There is no security outside yourself	God is our security
There is no way	There is a way; with God there is always a way
There is no wrong answer	Everything is right
There is nothing I can't do	I can achieve everything
There is nothing more	Complete
There is nothing that can stop you	All is in your favor
There is nothing wrong	Everything is perfect
There is nothing wrong with failure	You will succeed; learn from every experience
There is nothing you can't do, be or have	You can do, be and have it all
There will be no end	It will continue
These are scary times	With change comes opportunities
They are on a witch-hunt	They are very curious

ADVANCED AWARENESS	CREATIVE CHOICE
They can do no wrong	They are perfect
They can't understand me	I believe in myself
They did this to me	I allowed
They don't stand a chance	I am victorious
They don't understand me	I believe in myself
They never take initiative	I shall joyfully begin
They owe me	I allowed _____
They showed up	I showed up
They think I'm crazy	I dream big
This food is to die for	This is so delicious
This is not a kid's game	This takes maturity and experience
This is not how it is supposed to be	It's supposed to be _____
This is not mine	This belongs to someone else
This is not your authentic truth	Your authentic truth is _____
This is so bad	Wow; let's pray about it; let's choose again
This is to die for	This is wonderful
This sucks	I desire _____; I prefer _____
Through the dark	Ready to see the light; ready for inspiration
Tickled to death	I'm so happy
Time is money	My energy is worth money
Time will heal all wounds	Have faith and joyfully let go; let God
To no end	Continuing on
Too good to be true	Wondrous; miraculous; amazing
Too late	Life is progressing according to plan
Tough break	I experienced contrast

ADVANCED AWARENESS	CREATIVE CHOICE
Toughest moments	Opportunity to shine
Trial, error, and defeat	Learning from experience
Try not to	Try _____
Unadulterated magic	Pure magic
Unbroken wholeness	Complete
Unconditional love	Perfect love; pure love; agape love
Undeniable truth	Absolute truth; proven truth
Under the circumstances	As it stands now
Under the gun	Focus and finish
Under the weather	Please rest; I allow myself to stay home and rest
Under your breath	Quietly
Undesirable circumstances	What I now desire is
Undivided attention	Complete attention
Undivided good	Total good
Unexpected ways	Surprising ways
Unlimited abundance	Continual abundance
Unlimited potential	Vast potential
Unlimited power	Perfect power; continual power
Unmessable with	At peace
Unspoken of	New possibility
Until I am blue in the face	Until it's done
Use no medicine	Use energy
Vain imaginings	Illusions
Wage no more wars	Be at peace with
Wage war on	Share my opinion with

ADVANCED AWARENESS	CREATIVE CHOICE
Waiting for the other shoe to drop	Halfway there
Wake up from the nightmare	Start living by design
Way too fast	Please slow down
We all have our faults	We are perfect as we are; God made us as we are
We are in luck	Miracles are real; God's favor is on me; thanks God
We can't control our thoughts	We can control our words
We won't take no for an answer	Please say yes
Weapons of mass destruction	The most powerful option
Weighed down	Overpowered
Weight loss	My ideal weight is _____
What a coincidence	What a coordinated manifestation; divine order; serendipity
What else can go wrong	Everything is all right
What is the problem/trouble	How may I help
What is wrong with me	What can I do to improve
What is wrong with you	Help me understand your situation
What you fear will get you	Like attracts like; where focus goes energy flows
When I die	One day in the future
When I have a moment	Now; I plan it for _____
When in doubt	When you have questions
When it comes to an end	I choose now to _____
When pigs fly	Is it so; really
When push comes to shove	I always
When things don't work out	Everything will work out

ADVANCED AWARENESS	CREATIVE CHOICE
Whether you see it or not	It is there; have faith; believe
Who do you think you are	You are a child of God
Who has the time	I'm fully occupied
Why am I missing it	I am yet to understand
Why can't we	We can; we shall be; let us
Why don't we	We can; we shall be; let us
Why don't you	Will you; let us; how about
Why not	Absolutely
Why should we spend the money	I love to spend money
Will you not _____	Will you _____
Within the limits	Achievable; my parameters are _____
Without a doubt	Sure; certain
Without a time limit	Proceed at your leisure
Without attachment	Free
Without blinking	Steady; complete focus
Without difficulty	Light and easy
Without fear	Confident; peaceful
Without further delay	Now; immediately; right away
Without hesitation	Now
Without hierarchy	Equality
Without offense	Here is a suggestion
Without question	Absolutely
Without restrictions	Free
Without struggle	Easily
Without the slightest difficulty	Easily
Without wavering	Steadfast

ADVANCED AWARENESS	CREATIVE CHOICE
Without worry	Light and easy
Work hard	Work diligently
Work hard and get rich	Riches are a gift from God
Working hard	Working smart
Working my tail off	Putting a lot of energy into it
World filled with fear	World full of variety
Worry about	Have faith in God's plan
Worst enemy	It's all me
Worst mistake	Special opportunity
Worst-case scenario	Less than favorable; least desirable
Worth fighting for	Of great value
Would you mind	Can you please
Wrestle it to the ground	Complete it
You are a loser	Call forth your greatness
You are completely crazy	You are unique
You are crazy	Good for you; good on you
You are fooling yourself	You have high hopes
You are going to fail	With God all things are possible
You are impossible	You are something
You are just kidding/fooling yourself	You have high hopes
You are killing it	You are doing an excellent job
You are losing	Stay the course
You are merely	You are _____
You are never going to believe this	I am really excited to share this with you
You are never going to look at this again	It's only once
You are never satisfied	Can you appreciate it

ADVANCED AWARENESS	CREATIVE CHOICE
You are nobody	You are yet to be known; you are a child of God
You are pathetic	Cheer up
You bring out the worst in me	You really activate my emotions
You broke my heart	I had a different desired outcome
You can't _____	You can _____
You can't afford to _____	Be focused
You can't afford to listen to them	Stay your course
You can't fail	You will succeed
You can't have everything in this life	With God all things are possible
You can't lead from behind	Be confident
You can't lose	You can only win
You can't miss it	You will definitely see it
You could not possibly _____	Can you _____
You don't know	Please listen
You don't know what you don't know	Keep learning
You don't look well	Rest a bit and you will be better and better
You don't understand	Please understand; allow me to explain
You have my undivided attention	You have my complete attention
You have no idea	It was amazing; please understand
You have no power over that	Keep your positive attitude
You have nothing to lose	You have everything to gain
You have to be realistic	Dream bigger
You may never in your life	There is always a possibility
You may not be happy with _____	You will be happy with _____
You need not worry	All is well

ADVANCED AWARENESS	CREATIVE CHOICE
You needn't strive nor worry	God is in control
You never know	There is always a possibility
You never listen	Please listen
You sabotaged me	I am still seeking _____
You understand, don't you	The idea is _____
You will fail	With God all things are possible
You will never amount to much	Keep at it; success is yours
You will never do it	I hope you surprise me
You will never get it	It is currently beyond you
You will never succeed	Focus your energy and you will succeed
You won't be disappointed	You will be overjoyed
You won't believe this	Prepare for a surprise
Your luck won't last	Prepare, focus, and finish

TRANSFORMATIONAL VOCABULARY: WORDS

ADVANCED AWARENESS	CREATIVE CHOICE
Accident	By God's and my design
Amiss	Ready to be perfected; ready to be made right
Anti-aging	Stay youthful
Battle	Do your best and expect victory
Bemoaning	Ready to find greatness in it
Blameless	Perfect; righteous
Boring	Ready to create excitement
Boundless	Free
Braindead	Ready for enlightenment
Brainfog	It will come to me
Breathtaking	Life-giving; breath-giving
Bummer	I understand
But	And; however; yet
Ceaseless	Continual; constant
Chill	Relax
Close-minded	Honoring himself/herself
Countless	So many; vast
Curse	Pray against
Daredevil	Risktaker
Deadline	Set target date/time; goal
Deal-breaker	Obstacle
Death	Passing on; transition
Deathless	Eternal
Debt-free	Financially sound; abundant
Declutter	Organize

ADVANCED AWARENESS	CREATIVE CHOICE
Defeat	Yet to call in victory
Defeated	Ready to stand strong
Despair	Contrast
Despite	Anyway
Difficult	Challenging
Disagreeable	Yet to agree
Disastrous	Can use some love and improvement
Disillusioned	Temporarily sad
Distress	Desiring help
Dreadful	Currently seeking excitement
Effortless/Effortlessly	Light and easy
Endless	Continual; continuing
Endlessly	Continuous
Extraordinary	Super; fantastic; amazing; wonderful
Faults	Individuality; unique perfection
Fear-based	Illusion; ready for faith
Fear-free	Trust in God
Fearless/Fearlessly	Courageously; steadfast faith; content; faith-filled
Fearlessness	Courage
Fight	Do your best and expect victory
Flawless	Perfect
Flawlessness	Grace
Forget	Remember
Forgotten	Yet to be remembered
Formless	Expanse
Frightfully	In awe; respectfully

ADVANCED AWARENESS	CREATIVE CHOICE
Hate	Yet to accept
Hell-bent	Determined
Hinder	Slow
Hindrance	Temporary slowing; borders
Ill-will	Purposely against
Immovable	Steadfast
Immutable	Be heard
Impossible	Possible
Imprisonment	Temporary detention
Improbable	There is always a chance
Inadequate	Accept a better standard
Inadvertently	I had a different intention
Incompatible	Different
Inconceivable	Beyond grasp
Incorruptible	Honest; trustworthy; steadfast
Indeed	By grace
Indestructible	Perfect; remains intact; sturdy
Indifference	All equal
Inevitably	For sure; certain
Inexhaustible	Continuous
Infinite	Continuous; forevermore; ever expanding
Informal	Casual
Infuriates	Excites
Inharmonious	Allow harmony
Innumerable	Abundance of
Inseparable	Connected

ADVANCED AWARENESS	CREATIVE CHOICE
Intention	Total confidence; absolute focus
Invaluable	Of great worth; very valuable
Invariably	Always; certainly
Invincible	Perfect; remains intact; all-powerful; strong
Irresistible	Attractive; magnetic; inviting; appealing
Irritated	Off
Judgement	Acceptance
Lately	Recently
Left-wing	Unique
Lifeless	Quiet
Limitation	Illusion
Limited	Yet to find better options
Limitless	Capable of all things; free; continuous
Luck	By God's and my design
Madness	Variety
Merely	Just
Mindless	Free flowing
Misery	Contrast
Mistake	Part of the plan
Misunderstood	Brilliant; yet to be understood
Must	Let us
Need	Require
Neither	Either
Never	Yet to; done
Never-ending	Continual; continuing
Nevertheless	And yet

ADVANCED AWARENESS	CREATIVE CHOICE
No-brainer	Easy
Noiseless	Silent
Non-ending	Continual; continuing
Non-existent	Gone
No-nonsense	Straight forward
Non-resistant	Compliant; neutrality; flow
Nonsense	Illusion
Okay	good
Others	I
Outrageous	Out of the ordinary
Overwhelm	Extra stimulated; experiencing contrast
Pain	Sensation
Pain-free	Feel great; perfect health
Painless	Feel great; perfect health
Painstakingly	Detailed; thorough
Paralyzed	Yet to mobilize
Priceless	Valuable; worth much
Problem	Challenge
Problem-free	Happy; solution-oriented
Regardless	Anyway
Scarcely	Only
Seamless	Smooth
Selfless	Generous
Self-poisoning	Hard on yourself
Separation	Oneness
Should	Shall

ADVANCED AWARENESS	CREATIVE CHOICE
Sick	Returning to perfect health
Speechless	Silent
Starving	Feeling hungry
Stonewalling	Standing firm
Stress-free	Easy; calm; relaxed
Stressless	Easy; calm; relaxed
Suffering	Temporarily challenged; transitioning
Susceptible	Stand firm
Terrible/Terribly	Very; intense; strong; super
Terror	Ready to see the glory
Timeless	Forevermore
Tireless	Energized
Trial	Learning experience
Trouble-free	Flowing light and easy
Unadulterated	Pure
Unaffected	Pure; calm
Unanswered	Yet waiting
Unattainable	Yet to be achieved
Unavailable	Occupied
Unaware	Yet to understand; asleep
Unbelievable	Surprising; it is believable
Unbounded	Free flowing
Unbreakable	Permanent
Unbroken	Whole; complete
Uncanny	Amazing
Unceasing	Continuous

ADVANCED AWARENESS	CREATIVE CHOICE
Unchallenged	Simple
Unchangeable	Set; steadfast; constant
Unchanging	Steady; remains the same
Uncommon	Rare
Unconditional	Perfect; free
Unconditioned	Free thinking
Unconscious	Subconscious
Uncover	Open; discover
Undeniable	True; for sure
Underdog/slumdog	Less favored
Underestimated	Surprised
Undiscovered	Secret; hidden; ready to be found
Undisturbed	At peace; preserved; at rest; calm
Undivided	Whole; complete
Undone	Put together; opened
Undoubtedly	Absolutely
Unearthly	Heavenly
Uneasy	I desire to calm myself
Unending	Continual; continuing; forevermore
Unerring	Always correct
Unexpected	Surprising; new; miraculous
Unexpressed	Secret; ready to be shared
Unfailing	Dependable; continuous; secure; successful
Unfamiliar	New
Unfettered	Free
Unfold	Open up

ADVANCED AWARENESS	CREATIVE CHOICE
Unfolding	Opening
Unforeseen	Surprising
Unforgettable	Memorable
Unfortunately	Plans are changed
Unhappy	Ready for happiness; welcoming new possibilities
Unheard of	New possibility
Unhindered	Perfect; free
Unknowing	New
Unknown	New; mystery
Unleash	Free; allow
Unless	When
Unlimited	Vast; abundant; wide open; continual
Unlock	Open
Unmeasurable	Vast
Unmistakable	For sure; recognizable
Unmoved	Still; steadfast
Unnecessary	Elected; by choice; optional
Unprecedented	New experience
Unreal	Imaginary; amazing
Unrealistic	Expecting a miracle; That is a different perspective.
Unrestricted	Clear
Unseen	Hidden
Unselfish	Generous
Unsinkable	Stay afloat
Unstoppable	Continuing
Unsure	Yet to be certain

ADVANCED AWARENESS	CREATIVE CHOICE
Untapped	Brand-new
Untethered	Free
Untethered	Free
Until	Temporarily on hold; for
Unused	At rest
Unusual	Unique
Unwanted	Less desired; I prefer _____
Unwavering	Constant; steadfast
Unwilling	Passing on it
Unwobbling	Grounded; steadfast
Unworthy	Deserving better
Upsetting	Opportunity for alignment
Want	Choose; prefer; desire; seek
War	Peace
Warrior	A light
Warrior-prince(ss)	A light
Without	With
Worry-wart	Super focused on one thing

Please encourage us by adding your empowering conscious word choices to this list by sending an email to: ask@receivejoy.com

ABOUT RECEIVE JOY

Carisa Jones and Sylvia Lehmann founded Receive Joy together in 2017 as an answer to the ongoing question from Carisa's clients: What books do you recommend for me to read to understand the Power of the Universe and the Power of our words? As Carisa searched for printed material that truly explains in positive words how our thoughts and our words energetically create our life and our health, a solution was born: Receive Joy is a unique publishing company with a greater vision **using only positive words to encourage happiness, health, and wealth while living a purposeful, fulfilled, and focused life aligned with the Fruit of the Spirit.**

Receive Joy's books are written and published in Naples, Florida, and include materials focusing on creating and living a life by design with love and joy while bettering yourself and humanity.

Products include print books, eBooks, journals, workbooks, audio recordings containing inspirations, meditation and exercises, Joy Talks, devotionals, Inspiration Cards, online classes, and coaching. Receive Joy is here to encourage you to pick up your pen and script your life by design, to focus on your dreams and your purpose, make better choices to improve your life and give you mindful solutions. We believe that we all are born with the opportunity to focus on the good that is abundant everywhere.

Ask And You Shall Receive is Receive Joy's first book, published in 2017 and now an international bestseller. This book combines the Power of Positive Words with the Power of Attraction and Faith to help encourage you to create and define a direction and plan for your life. Our Nine Step Method to Consciously Create empowers you to become a new, more powerful, focused and loved, aware, and connected you. This is the secret beyond *The Secret*.

Please refer to the next pages for more information about Receive Joy's available products and events.

Contact Carisa and Sylvie when you are interested to learn more. Visit www.receivejoy.com. Subscribe to our newsletter to continue your receiving of positive awareness. Please share your email address with us and we'll share with you empowering strategies to live a life by design. Send us a message directly to ask@receivejoy.com or text to US cell phone number (239) 450-1240. Like and follow Receive Joy on Facebook: www.facebook.com/ReceiveJoy. Follow Receive Joy on Instagram: www.instagram.com/receivejoy. Subscribe to our YouTube channel (Receive Joy) and enjoy free Joy Talks.

Receive Joy commits to pray for 2,000 likeminded individuals and help them to be the best version of themselves by personally connecting and holding the high frequency of glory for each and every one of our Mastermind members. Be part of our elite group of 2,000. We welcome you to personally contact us.

We are happy to hear from you and receive your positive feedback, inspiration, and miracle stories!

MILLION TRUE MILLIONAIRES

MTM is a social network, bringing together an international community of positive, purpose-driven individuals who strive for growth, contribution, and love.

This is your personal invitation to join the MTM community for an annual fee of $225 to:

- ♥ Have access to other members—what a joy it is to have like-minded, purpose-driven individuals to connect with

- ♥ Share your visions and askings and start receiving

- ♥ Market your products and services

- ♥ Find new business partners and make friends

- ♥ Receive mentorship from proven successful individuals

- ♥ Browse the library to find empowering videos, eBooks, and links to amazing websites and blogs

- ♥ Receive regular newsletters and invitations to webinars in which we share valuable information to help you and your business grow

- ♥ Receive community and encouragement. Our goal is for all MTM members to succeed together as we encourage each other along the way. We all grow abundantly in happiness, health, and wealth

- ♥ Receive love and prayer. All our members are constantly prayed over

Tap into all of these benefits and become part of this success network. People who are successful have one thing in common: They believe that they can succeed and so they do. MTM is here to support its members. Together, we share in each other's greatness. We each wish to experience and spread community, love, kindness, positivity, personal growth, peace on earth, bettering of mankind, charity, giving, and receiving.

In MTM's ever growing and expanding library:

- ♥ Every Monday at 12:30 p.m. we have a member zoom call: the MTM Mentoring Hour. Join us live every Monday 12:30 p.m. EST on zoom (invitation comes to your email inbox with MTM membership) or watch the recording archived in the library section of MTM. Please email ask@receivejoy.com for a free trial-session

- ♥ Receive Joy recorded more than 12 Joy Talks (about 10 minutes each) on different topics. Be inspired!

- ♥ Listen to nine advanced Receive Joy Trainings (about 1 hour each)

- ♥ Enjoy all the recorded Miracle Group Meetings (about 2 hours each)

- ♥ Read the inspirational articles Receive Joy has published and listen to podcasts

- ♥ And much more

Join our international society and have access to the Receive Joy library growing your happiness, health, and wealth:

www.milliontruemillionaires.com

When you or a friend join MTM, Receive Joy offers you a **60-minute free personalized mentoring session**. Once you have joined, please email ask@receivejoy.com to set up an appointment.

With blessings in Abundance, your MTM Family A Family of Wealth—We trust in God!

MIRACLE GROUP MEETINGS

A few years ago, a group of friends decided to come together and practice positive intentions. During our meetings we share positive words and energy, we learn, listen, and refine our manifesting skills. We are likeminded individuals who help and encourage each other, second our askings, and have open-minded conversations. We let each other know our desires for what we are wishing to receive through the habit of manifestation, and then in the following meetings we share our manifested miracles while encouraging each other with great love and gratitude. We practice collective intent in harmony with other energetic positive minds.

We meet every two weeks for most of the year and these meetings have become a place for meaningful friendships, support, inspirations, respect, love, acceptance of all, reminders, joy, and rediscovering the truth. This is our Miracle Group. We embrace with optimism that we are a powerful part of a larger whole.

Many of the stories in Receive Joy's books are manifestations from the Miracle Group.

We invite you to **join us for free!** We meet every second Tuesday in Naples, Florida. We also use zoom for everyone to enjoy the meeting in their own home. Email ask@ receivejoy.com to be added to the invitation list with the zoom link. We record the meetings for listening pleasure anytime. The recordings are available on Receive Joy's YouTube channel (see page 154.)

EXPERIENCE A BEAUTIFUL LIFE

Come and live God's philosophy of good. Be a child again and play with us at one of our retreats. We offer around five retreats per year where we experience joy all day long. For more information contact us: ask@receivejoy.com

AVAILABLE FROM RECEIVE JOY

All products are directly available from Receive Joy: ask@receivejoy.com or call/text (239) 450-1240. You may also order from the Receive Joy Store, accessible via **www.receivejoy.com** or scan the **QR Code**. Use the code FREESHIPPINGUSA during checkout and shipping is paid for by Receive Joy.

SCAN ME

ASK AND YOU SHALL RECEIVE Series

Ask And You Shall Receive (Print, eBook, and Audiobook)

Daily Asking Journal

Inspiration Notebook

Ask And You Shall Receive Meditation (Audio recording)

CONNECT TO THE LIGHT Series

Connect To The Light
(Print, eBook, and Audiobook)

Focus Wheel Workbook

Focus Target Workbook

Connect To The Light Meditation
(Audio recording)

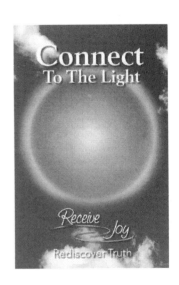

BLESSED BY THE TONGUE Series

Blessed By The Tongue

Every Word Matters

Speak Transformation Workbook

Receive Beautiful Words (Audio recording)

RECEIVE INSPIRATION Series

Receive Inspiration

Receive Joy Every Day

Receive Inspiration, Card Deck

Receive Inspiration (Audio recording)

Other Products by Receive Joy:

Receive Joy Mug

Receive Joy Bag

Receive Joy Notepad

DAILY FOCUS ACTIONS

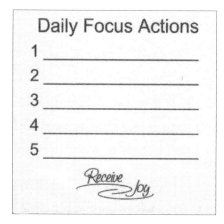

Use these handy *Daily Focus Actions* sticky notes to keep your focus on the five things you can do as a Ten Star Experience. Stick it on the cover of your *Daily Asking Journal*, pray over the content and leave the rest up to God.

$5 per pack of 25 sticky notes, directly available from Receive Joy

EXCLUSIVE TITLES BY RECEIVE JOY

Live By Design

Waves of Abundance

Immense Freedom

Receive Miracles

The 7 Absolutes

30 Days of Asking

30 Ways of Asking

Believe and Receive

Let's Pray Workbook

Receive Joy from the Beginning

Wash Your Heart

Start Asking

Ask Yourself

Ask And Receive More

Receive Wealth: Grow Rich

Receive Joy for Teens

Experience A Beautiful Life

The Art of Changing

The Tree of Life

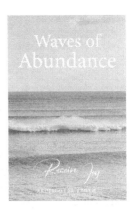

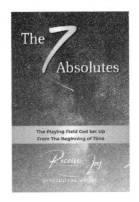

Please contact us at ask@receivejoy.com when you are interested in any of our titles from the exclusive list.

RECEIVE JOY LESSONS

Change your life for $1—one lesson at a time. Enjoy these inspiring, empowering thoughts for $1 each.

1. The Pivoting Point: Own It

2. Start Asking: How To Ask

3. I Declare: The Power Of Asking

4. Start Receiving: How To Receive

5. The Power Of Daily Journaling: Pick Up Your Pen

6. The Tree Of Life: One Absolute Power

7. Life's Three Illusions: Control, Security & Pleasing Others

8. The Power Of Receiving & Giving: Contribution & Charity

9. God-Trading: Be Of God's World

10. I Allowed: The Art Of Allowing

11. Oneness: See The Perfection In All

12. Yes: The Power Of Yes

13. Live In The Glory: Experience Your Greatness

14. Stop Blaming: It's All Me

15. Stop It: The #1 Piece Of Advice

16. Hold Your Tongue: Receive Your Gift

17. Count It All Joy: Experience A Beautiful Life

18. Be Aware: He Who Has Ears, Let Him Hear

19. Mastering Defensiveness: Be Still

20. The Art Of Changing: Out With The Old, In With The New

21. Walk By Faith: God Is Our Supply

22. Beautiful Words: Call In Your Beautiful Life

23. Hope: The Expected Outcome (Anchored In God's Promises)

24. Be Calm: Align Your Head With Your Heart

More lessons are added continuously. Email ask@receivejoy.com to receive a full list of available lessons (over 150).

Each lesson comes with mind-opening exercises, a call to action, Bible verses to memorize, believable affirmations and powerful prayers. These eBooks (pdf) are 5 to 20 pages and are available for $1/each.

RECEIVE JOY ONLINE CLASSES

Live By Design

Enjoy ten empowering lessons: 1. Goal Setting, 2. The Nine Steps To Consciously Create, 3. I Declare: Asking, 4. The Power Of Your Word: Every Word Matters, 5. The Power Of The Pen: Journaling, 6. Own It All: It's All Me, 7. The Seed, 8. Be It To Attract It, 9. Meditation, Incantation, Affirmations, 10. The Tree of Life, including Bonus Videos
$44

Let's Begin

In this online class, Receive Joy helps you start your walk in using your conscious creation power. The videos contain step-by-step tutorials of all the exercises presented in *Ask And You Shall Receive.*
$37

Ask And You Shall Receive

An in-depth training on Receive Joy's Nine Steps To Consciously Receive as presented in the book *Ask And You Shall Receive* with many powerful exercises.
$197

Please email ask@receivejoy.com for more information on the online classes and to receive the link to a training of your choice when you are ready to take the next step to own your life!

ASK AND YOU SHALL RECEIVE

The Power of Positive Words
+ the Law of Attraction
+ God
= Your Light and Easy Life!

This is "the secret beyond the secret"! This book will help encourage you to create and define a direction and plan for your life. I wish to share my Nine Step Method to empower everyone to feel the freedom of a light and easy life. Open your heart and your mind and journey with me to a new and more powerful, focused and loved, aware and connected You.

$15 (Amazon $20), ISBN: 978-0-9988484-8-8

Chapter 7

THE POWER OF THE WORD

"In the beginning was the word. And the word was with God and the word was God."
—John 1:1 (NIV)

Besides forming man, God spoke everything that is into existence. He uses words. **All creation was, is, and will be spoken or written into existence.**

The Power Of The Word

"And God **said**, 'Let there be light,' and there was light."
—Genesis 1:3 (NIV)

God left us *The Holy Bible*. It is a book which, when opened, is full of only one thing: words. The Bible is our manual to this life experience. Every year, it is the number one best-selling book in the world. It supersedes all other book sales by such a great margin, because humankind's powerful and universal desire to know God and His Word is continual.

The word trumps the thought. At a seminar, I had the privilege to walk across hot coals. And even though my mind knew they were hot and my body was questioning my mind, I successfully crossed the coals because of my chanting and anchoring positive words of "Yes, I can. I am walking on cool moss." When my mind questioned the ability of my body to achieve it, my words trumped my mind.

64

65

Ask And You Shall Receive

"Not what goes into the mouth defiles a man; but **what comes out of the mouth**, this defiles a man."
—Matthew 15:11 (NKJV)

When my 91-year-old friend and yoga instructor was ready to live in a nursing home, we went through all his important documents. He chose me to be executor of his will. I talked with him about his long-term insurance policy and asked him to tell me the story of when he bought it.

His words were, "The sales person told me that I will most likely *never* use it, *but* it is good to have anyway." He bought the policy and paid the annual premiums for 35 years, which amounted to roughly $350,000. The policy stated that in the case that the policyholder moves to a nursing home, the first 60 days rent will be paid by the policyholder before the insurance begins coverage. My friend passed on after 59 days in the nursing home.

88

The Power Of Using Positive Words

" . . . For the mouth speaks what the heart is full of."
—Luke 6:45 (NIV)

Are our words defining us? Are we conscious and aware of our own words? Do we understand the power of our own words? Are we encouraging ourselves and others with every word we speak?

Words come from organized thoughts so it is important to write down our words for organization. A study by Dr. Matthias Mehl and his team at the University of Arizona found that women and men speak an average of 16,000 words per day. The Laboratory of Neuro Imaging estimates an average person has roughly 70,000 thoughts per day.

89

---

1. **Connect**: Plug into God's Almighty **Gift**, the Power of the Universe, and discover your life's purpose.

2. **Declare**: Be clear about what you are truly seeking and ask for it.

   Have **Faith,** focus, and be courageous.

3. **Dominate**: Receive your inheritance and put on your crown.

   Believe.

4. **Be calm**: **Align** your head with your heart.

   Have **Peace**.

5. **Take action**: Focus on your breath and let the "how" be up to God.

   Let Him wow us with the "how." He does it.

   Experience God's **Glory**.

6. **Lead with love**: Let us **love ourselves first**.

   Have **Grace**.

7. **Bless everyone** and **everything** with **love and gratitude.**

   Have **Mercy**.

8. **Expect the miracle in every moment**. Know the **Truth**.

   Be conscious of what you create and allow yourself to receive your desires.

9. **Have fun and celebrate**: Enjoy your creation and rejoice.

   Trust God.

Dear Father God,
You are the light of my life.
Thank You for this perfect day.
Thank You for this perfect moment.
Thank You for creating me in Your image.
I accept that I am Your child and that I hold Your creation power.
Thank You for Your wisdom.
Thank You for allowing me plenty of time to accomplish everything.
Most of all, I am thankful that You are always with me and
are my greatest support.
My life is balanced and flows light and easy.
I recognize the good that is abundant everywhere.
I am calm. I have a peaceful heart.
I am Love. I love myself so that I can have love for others.
I find it easy to love myself and others.
Love flows through me and touches everyone in my life.
My love is so great that it surrounds all and everything.
I constantly create great thoughts of love and joy.
I am joy. I am a true blessing. Keep me cheerful so that I may serve You.
I am grateful that I know the truth.
I am grateful that I have a definite life's purpose.
I am grateful that I use beautiful positive words that create.
It is my intention to speak with clarity, happiness, and love.
May every thought I think and every word I speak be full of Your perfect love.
I am grateful that I am incredibly successful and that wealth and abundance
come from everywhere. Money flows frequently and abundantly.
I rejoice in You Jesus.
With love, gratitude and happiness,
Your loving child

Receive Joy

WHAT READERS THINK OF
ASK AND YOU SHALL RECEIVE

"I completed the read of your book. Impressive work!!! Much of this I studied over decades. So many of your written words feel very comfortable to me, a little overwhelming, yes, yet very comfortable. The water and words chapter was a profound reminder of how much our words impact our lives. I guess I know what I will be observing for the next two weeks. I am excited to begin this journey. I did realize that something was off-center with my thoughts, emotions, and words the last few years, and perhaps forever they were off, yet I feel empowered that correcting this is a very achievable process. I shall demand my crown and take my proper place in the universe soon enough. Thank you for the wake-up call. As I am sure you already figured out, few could motivate me to open my mind, heart, and soul to take on such a wonderful and rewarding journey. God bless."
—David C., Texas

"Great read and excellent message! Real life examples gave me goose bumps as I thought of my own personal experiences. I can't wait to read the next book!"
—Joshua R., North Carolina

"It is inspiring, powerful and filled with love. With so many challenging things happening in the world right now, this book is a joy to read. It helps you focus on what is truly important in life and lets you get back to you."—Ann H., Florida

"I have read this book four times and I keep it in sight, on my nightstand, as a reminder of all of the positive joy. It's a must read!"—Donna H.

"I'm almost done with the book and have started the journal as well, and listening to the CD while I drive...Today I sat at my desk and did some of the exercises in the book and it became clear for the first time in my whole life that my divine mission is to create beauty for others through my creative gifts and talents. It's the first time ever that I've stepped into and named my calling. So grateful to have this focus and bloom it out into the world! The feeling is fantastic! Thank you!!!"—Tiffany R.

"This book was a delight. It was easy to read and follow and the actions to follow are simple! So often reading this type of content can get complicated. The authors broke down the material in a beautifully simplistic way! I highly recommend this book and have so enjoyed it!"—Heidi C., Georgia

"This is such an inspiring book. I've read it twice so far and have gifted copies to 10 people who are an important part of my life. Anyone can receive a life filled with joy. It's just a matter of learning how to ask."—Jan Z.

"This awesome book came at the perfect time in my life. Joy Joy Joy"
—Deborah G., Florida

"Simple steps to change your life: *Ask and You Shall Receive* is obviously written from a place of Passion, Knowledge, and Experience. The numerous real-life examples you will read (many times, if you are like me) balance well with the How-To sections and the positivity that courses throughout the pages infuses the book with an energy of purposeful pace that also gives abundant time to absorb and apply the ideas and exercises. From a personal point of view, the contents of this book have already begun working in my life. I am practicing what is prescribed and seeing results. I found it to speak clearly to me. If you have a penchant for practical solutions and clear instructions it will certainly be satisfied. The precepts and ideas in the book are familiar from the works of teachers like Wayne Dyer, Caroline Myss, and Ram Dass, yet they are presented in such a way as to be brand new. No one, in my extensive study of both spiritual practices and storytelling, has focused so clearly on the Word, the all-important Logos. Receive Joy's stated goal is a book that is "light and easy." I found it to be tremendously so! It has Air, Space, Peace, and Love infused in it. This book was a great gift that came at the perfect time in my life."—Joey M., North Carolina

To read more five-star reviews, visit *Ask And You Shall Receive* on amazon.com and scroll to the comment section.

SCAN ME

ASK AND YOU SHALL RECEIVE MEDITATION

Enjoy this 20-minute *Ask And You Shall Receive Meditation* in all positive words—listen to the truth about yourself and receive inspiration.

$5
UPC: 098867225629

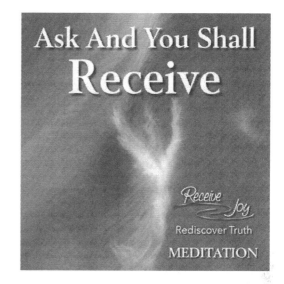

This source of light is God's Almighty Power. This beautiful, continual, abundant power. It is formulated from love. It is light and life. It is warm. It is comforting. It is here to support and comfort me. It embraces me. I know the light is here to love and support me. I know the light is here to help and comfort me. It is awesome and full of power.

This Almighty Power is abundant. It is free and equally available to everyone.

I recognize abundance everywhere. The Universe pulls from all resources of all existence. I understand the Almighty Power. I tap into all the abundance. I am so grateful that I am part of the wonderful, great abundance that all humanity comes from. I choose to connect to this power.

I can see this beautiful, powerful light over my head. It looks perfect. This beautiful light is abundant. I welcome this beautiful, perfect light. This beautiful light is the Almighty Power coming through me. It enters into the crown of my head and as it makes its way through my body, I relax even more.

I am calmer and calmer. I am perfect. I am the child of God. I am created in His image. I hold His creation power. I know His mercy. I hold His wisdom. I tap into His free gift of abundance and create my perfect life every day.

The light fills me. I am fulfilled. As it comes into the crown of my head, it balances my brain. It helps to focus my mind and my thoughts. I think positive thoughts that attract what I desire. I use the enormous power of my mind. I have the power to welcome only the thoughts that bless me. I have the power to turn away all opposing thoughts. I constantly create great thoughts of love and joy.

I know that what I focus on I receive more of. I am completely focused. By faith, I declare all my actions before I take them. With grace, I visualize the outcome. I declare the exact outcome. I reach my desires fast and accurately. I write great plans for my life. I am clear about what I intend for each day. I write down what I welcome in each day. I ask for my desires with great precision. I love to declare in exact detail.

I speak only beautiful words that create

DAILY ASKING JOURNAL

Live by Design!

To make your life light and easy, let us put the Nine Step Method into daily action by using the *Daily Asking Journal*. This Journal will help connect you with the Power of the Universe and enable you to collect and compile all your asking intentions in one place. This personal journal for your focused thoughts and positive words supports you to raise your awareness, while having an organized platform to consciously create and record your positive, happy, light, and easy life. Script your life, keep on asking God, and be a new wineskin.

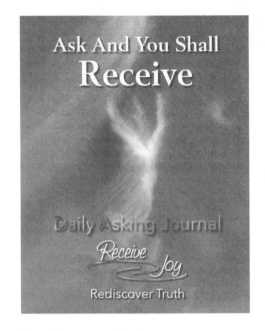

$10 (Amazon $12)
ISBN: 978-0-9988484-0-2

HOW TO JOURNAL DAILY

1. Fill in today's date.

2. Read the daily inspiration and Bible verse. Be blessed, inspired, and receive joy!

3. Thank God and list whatever you are grateful for in the box labeled **I am grateful for**. Please include people, events, and circumstances. What aspects in your life are you thankful for? What went well today? Remember to include personal features and emotions. Allow this list to grow and grow every day. Read through your accumulated gratitude and feel your spirit lifted as often as desired.

4. Take a Five Minute Couch Time (as described in Receive Joy's book *Ask And You Shall Receive* on page 232) during your day to ponder a specific question you have and listen to the inspired answers you receive, or take time now and reflect on your day. Ask yourself: **What may I do to allow more happiness and peace to flow into my life?** What additional consciousness and acceptance shall I welcome in for me to be God's new wineskin? Write your answer on the lines provided.

5. List one action that you will take in the next 24 hours to **celebrate this day**. Select something you find joyful and fun. Play your Game of Fun, roll the dice, and choose the rewarding activity you land on.

MY MONTHLY GOALS

My goals for the month of _____

_____
_____
_____
_____
_____
_____
_____
_____
_____
_____
_____
_____
_____
_____
_____
_____

I vividly see myself with my goals obtained and miracles created!

_____   _____
        Signature   Date

Date: _____

I now joyfully accept and appreciate the abundant life the Universe offers me.

I am grateful for:
_____
_____
_____
_____
_____

What may I do to allow more happiness and peace in my life?
_____
_____
_____

I have fun and celebrate this day by:
_____

I ask with focused intent for:
_____
_____
_____
_____
_____
_____ and more!

Why?
_____
_____
_____
_____
_____
_____

My gains and miracles created:
_____
_____
_____
_____
_____

1 _____
2 _____
3 _____
4 _____
5 _____

To God be the glory!   Thank you for my breath of life.   I rejoice always.

"Rejoice in the Lord always: and again I say, Rejoice."

—Philippians 4:4 (KJV)

❑ I read my Bible.
❑ I am connected to God.
❑ I meditated for 15 min.
❑ I edited my words three times.
❑ I prayed.
❑ I smile.

☺

second energy [ ]

137

Date: _____

**I am the co-creator of my own life and
I act with grace and mercy in all I do.**

I am grateful for:	What may I do to allow more happiness and peace in my life?
_____	_____
_____	_____
_____	_____
_____	**I have fun and celebrate this day by:**
_____	_____

I ask with focused intent for:	Why?
_____	_____
_____	_____
_____	_____
_____	_____
_____	_____
_____ and more!	_____

My gains and miracles created:	
_____	1 _____
_____	2 _____
_____	3 _____
_____	4 _____
_____	5 _____

To God be the glory!   Thank you for my breath of life.   I rejoice always.

"Jesus replied: 'Love the Lord your God with all your heart and with all your soul and with all your mind.'"

—Matthew 22:37 (NIV)

❑ I read my Bible.
❑ I am connected to God.
❑ I meditated for 15 min.
❑ I edited my words three times.
❑ I prayed.
❑ I smile.

☺

second energy [ ]

I declare that _____

_____

_____

My parameters:

1. _____
2. _____
3. _____
4. _____
5. _____
6. _____
7. _____
8. _____

Why?

- _____
- _____
- _____
- _____
- _____

Thank you God, Jesus, and Holy Spirit!

_____

and more!   second energy ☐

I declare that _____

_____

_____

My parameters:

1. _____

2. _____

3. _____

4. _____

5. _____

6. _____

7. _____

8. _____

Why?

- _____

- _____

- _____

- _____

- _____

Thank you God, Jesus, and Holy Spirit!

_____

and more!   second energy ☐

INSPIRATION NOTEBOOK

Live inspired!

The *Inspiration Notebook* is designed as a platform to create and record your inspirations and highlights, ideas and insights, goals and plans. Daily writing enables you to experience a purposeful life with clarity. Your continual plans of action and written insights guide you toward your goals and direct all focus on your target. Let this personal journal hold your ideas and goals.

The *Inspiration Notebook* is a tool to help you measure your continual growth and accomplishments. Pick up a pen, and script your life in your own hand.

$10 (Amazon $12)
ISBN: 978-0-9988484-5-7

Sample Pages:

JANUARY

WEEKLY GOALS

Week 1

Week 2

Week 3

Week 4

JANUARY

1   *I now joyfully accept and appreciate the abundant life the Universe offers me.*

2   *I am in perfect health. My body feels amazing.*

3   *I accept all the good around me.*

4   *I flow with all that life offers me in every moment.*

Let our *Inspiration Notebook* assist you in imagining, creating, recording, and remembering your miraculous life. This notebook is a tool to help you measure your continual growth and accomplishments.

 Now pick up a pen, and script your life in your own hand.

Start by filling in your **Divine Mission Statement**. What is your life about? Include your key values and words that describe you. Revisit and rewrite your Mission Statement as often as you desire.

Next, fill in your **Goals For This Year**. What do you wish to accomplish during the next 365 days? By signing the page, you consciously commit to a contract with yourself. This is an opportunity to hold yourself accountable to the standards and goals you call in. You may choose to obtain a second signature from your prayer/accountability partner.

> "Again, truly I tell you that if **two of you on earth agree about anything they ask for**, it will be done for them by my Father in heaven. For where two or three gather in my name, there am I with them."—Matthew 18:19-20

Out of your list of goals, pick the most important one. To keep your eyes on the victory, write your goal in the center of the bull's-eye on the **Focus Target** page. Fill in your additional goals according to their importance in the outer rings. After you have filled in the whole target, make a copy and place the sheet where it can be seen daily.

Simultaneously, it is beneficial to have goals in all important areas of your life. Live by design and fill in the rings of the eight Focus Targets following your GOALS FOR THIS YEAR-Target to enhance your clarity and focus. What are your ideals when it comes to these eight valuable areas:

- ♥ Happiness
- ♥ Health
- ♥ Wealth
- ♥ Love & Community
- ♥ Growth
- ♥ Spirituality
- ♥ Career
- ♥ Personal Space

We provided you with an overview of the **Nine Steps** to consciously create. Each month starts with a summary of a lesson as presented in *Ask And You Shall Receive*, followed by the opportunity to express

GOALS FOR THIS YEAR

I vividly see myself with my goals obtained and miracles created!

_____   _____
Signature   Date

GOALS FOR THIS YEAR _____

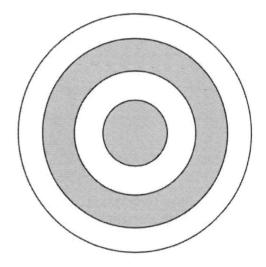

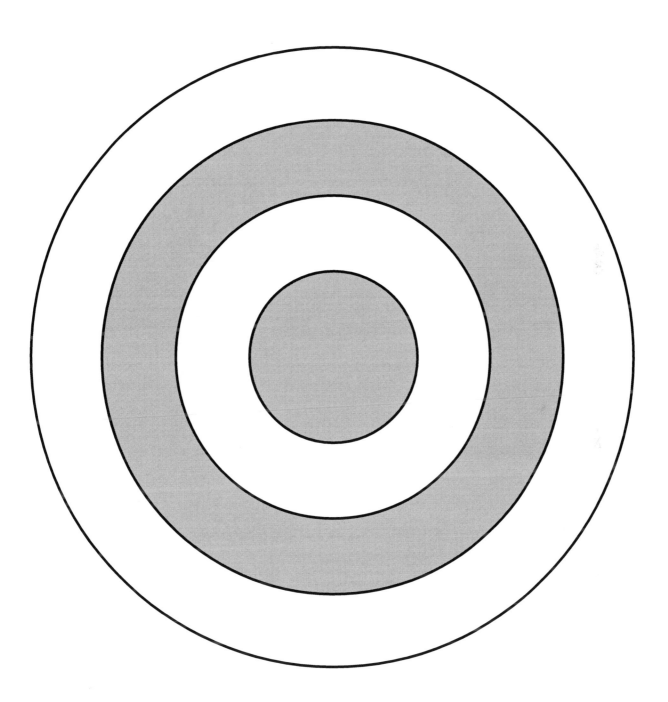

CONNECT TO THE LIGHT

We charge our cellphone, plug in the toaster and the hairdryer, let us also plug our life in first. Step one in the process of truly deciding to make changes in our life and begin living by design starts with the understanding that we are connected to the greatest Power Source there is—God. Let us consciously connect first and harness this power. Once we are connected, our life starts to flow.

Connect To The Light provides ways to maintain our connection to the light energy and to live by conscious design. Let us be heavenly-minded, yet of earthly use.

$20

ISBN: 978-0-9988484-1-9

Sample Pages:

CONTENTS

INTRODUCTION

When we place a cake mix in the oven, after we have combined together all the ingredients listed on the back, if the oven is still off, or if we turn it on after our mix has been in the oven for 30 minutes, the outcome is different than if we had precisely followed the baking instructions. The instructions generally recommend to turn the oven on **first**. It says "Step One: Preheat oven." To heat, the oven has to be plugged in and turned on for the cake mix to bake correctly into a cake. It is paramount to do Step One first. First connect: Plug in and turn on.

Welcome to Step One of Receive Joy's *Ask And You Shall Receive* Nine Step Method to Consciously Create. This book dives deeper into Step One: Connect. It contains many additional insights about **why** it is important to connect first, **ways** to connect, and ways to **stay connected** to the Light of God.

"Seek ye **first** the Kingdom of God and his righteousness; and all these things shall be added unto you."

—Matthew 6:33 (KJV)

Receive Joy has written *Connect To The Light* to guide and encourage a permanent and more personal connection with God and to help everyone take responsibility to live their life by conscious design. This is the point where we have to make a conscious decision: Are we of this world or of God's world? Are we aligning our will to God's will, surrendering completely, and living by intricate design? Let us understand that God is the Power of the Universe and we gain life in and through Him. *"Luck"* and *"co-incidence"* are fabrications of this world. Absolute power and divine order are the very fabric of God's supernatural plan. This book will help us to connect to this ultimate, mighty power source. God is the light.

"Part One: Connect!" explains in detail what it means to be connected to the light, why it is important to connect first, and what we can learn about ourself to spark the desire to live by design. By the end of Part One, everyone shall have discovered their current divine mission and trust in their all-knowing.

"Part Two: Stay Connected!" offers enlightening examples to establish a connection and stay connected to God, day by day, moment by moment.

Let us ask ourself to open our heart and consciousness to have God's light shine in and through us. Let us reach out into these new areas of understanding and welcome them in. Let us open our heart and our mind now and journey to a new and more powerful, focused and loved, light and easy, aware and **connected** YOU! Let us connect and live by design!

1

2

3

CONNECT TO THE LIGHT MEDITATION

We charge our cellphone, plug in the toaster and the hairdryer, let us also plug our life in first. We are connected to the greatest Power Source there is—God. Let us consciously connect first and harness this power. Once we are connected our life starts to flow.

1. Connect To The Light Meditation
2. Exercise: The Grand Doors Of My Life
3. Connect To The Light Prayer

$10
UPC: 098867227623

FOCUS WHEEL WORKBOOK

The *Focus Wheel Workbook* presents you with an easy exercise to engage your belief system, stay in a positive mindset, and pray into the solution. Receive Joy collected over 50 statements to help you think about excellent and praiseworthy things. Encourage yourself to increase your belief in all areas of life by expressing clarity and solid evidence in writing. This workbook also aids in believing in and focusing on your goals. Seek God first, focus on your greatness, and live by design.

$15 (Amazon $20)
ISBN: 978-0-9988484-9-5

Sample Pages:

YOUR GUIDE FOR USING THE FOCUS WHEEL WORKBOOK

"Let your eyes look straight ahead; fix your gaze directly before you."
—Proverbs 4:25 (NIV)

The *Focus Wheel Workbook* presents you with an easy exercise to engage your belief system, stay in a positive mindset, and pray into the solution.

Encourage yourself to increase your belief in all areas of life by expressing clarity and solid evidence in writing. As you increase your belief, the desired outcome is attainable. You are creating certainty to increase your belief and actively imprint your subconscious. Keep your eyes on the victory, build a solution-oriented mindset, and ultimately receive your desired goals. All the answers and solutions are in you already.

1. Choose a thought or belief you wish to increase. It may be a feeling that is outdated and you wish to update. The first step is to recognize and identify your current belief system. What thoughts do you repeatedly think? What sayings did you hear over and over growing

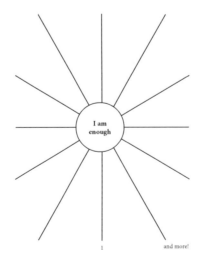

1   and more!

I am enough

Variations: I am good enough

♥ I am a child of God

♥ God loves me

♥ God gave me gifts and talents for my mission on earth

♥ I am perfect just as I am

♥ I am content

♥ God sustains me

♥ I always make the most of everything

♥ I am always growing and progressing

♥ I am enough and I always will be enough

♥ God gives me everything I require to succeed

♥ My family and friends love me as I am

♥ I know what it feels like to be enough

_____

_____

_____

_____

1

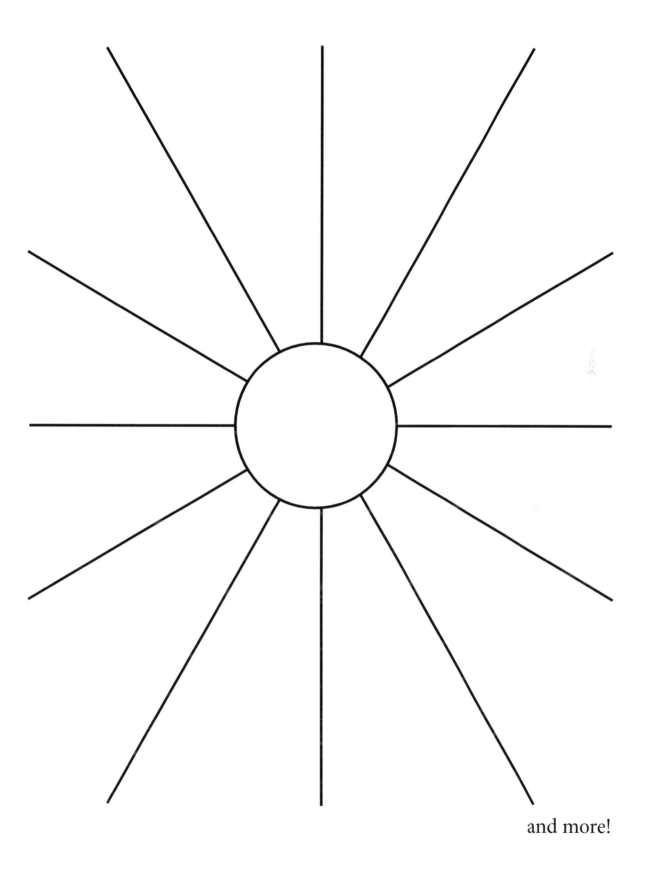

and more!

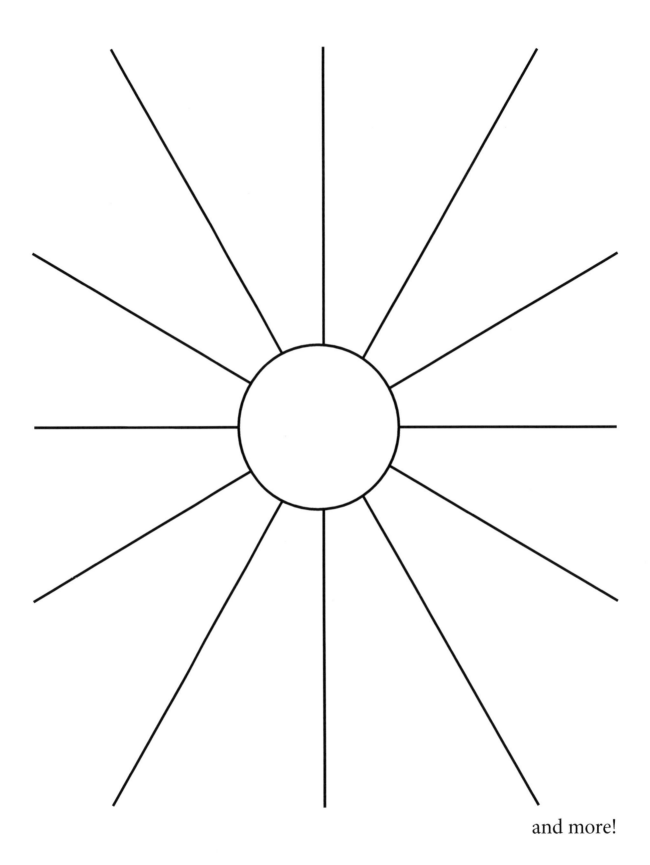

and more!

RECEIVE INSPIRATION

CD, $10
UPC: 098867227227

Receive Inspiration contains a mix of inspirations to open the mind to receive happiness, love, prosperity, well-being, growth, focus, and allowing. Receive Joy created this encouraging CD using only positive words so that we may consciously choose to remember our greatness. Let us cheer ourselves on! Be inspired!

Receive joy and open the mind and heart through positive blessed inspiration. Let us rediscover the truth of flow and allow.

- I now joyfully accept and appreciate the abundant life the Universe offers me.
- I flow with all that life offers me in every moment.
- I have all the resources I require. I am resourceful.
- I know that everything I focus on I receive more of.
- Divine love attracts all good.
- Today, I find a hundred reasons to feel good.
- I create miracles in every moment.
- My perfect life is full of abundance. I recognize abundance everywhere. I tap into all the abundance.
- I am in perfect health. My body feels amazing.
- I accept all the good around me.
- My life is light and easy.
- I reach all my goals easily.
- Divine love fills me and I express kindness, tenderness and compassion.
- I understand the Almighty Power.
- I am so grateful that I am part of the wonderful abundance that all humanity comes from.
- I have faith, I believe. My heart is at peace.
- I accept all truth and understanding.
- I am fulfilled. I know that my desires are taken care of.
- I can do everything and anything with God.

RECEIVE BEAUTIFUL WORDS

CD, $10
UPC: 098867227128

Every word is a creation. We can choose to create love, joy, gratitude, hope, compassion, mercy, praise and much more positivity with our words. Let us be conscious of the words we send out to achieve what we desire. Play Receive Beautiful Words to imprint ourselves and our environment with positive blessings. Listen and Receive Joy!

BEAUTIFUL WORDS
(Audio CD)

love	hug	explore
joy	evolving	nutritious
laugh	bliss	instantaneously
light	purple	complete
honesty	funny	adorable
purpose	affluent	encourage
friendly	thankful	change
right	sensible	emotion
wonderful	zest	reliable
positive	cherish	artistic
imagine	special	gentle
finish	magical	mighty
capable	industrious	pretty
inventive	give thanks	eagerness
smart	flowing	whole
valuable	achieving	robust
lead	ideas	far-sighted
fabulous	balance	already
rejoice	truly	cute
well	depth	I love you
meaningful	humorous	peaceful
unification	motivated	respectful
dream	intentions	versatile
healthy	radiance	zeal
prompt	here and now	gather
victorious	strong	happiness
precious	water	exquisite

RECEIVE JOY SERVICES

COACHING

Personal and Health Advancement. One-on-one coaching sessions (in person, via phone, Skype or Zoom) to assist you in formulating, clarifying, and reaching your goals as you increase your conscious awareness.

60 min., $100

Receive Joy is your accountability and prayer partner! Goal setting and prayer once/week

15 min., $25

MASTERMIND ALLIANCE

Learn how to mastermind. Receive Joy teaches you in four 1-hour meetings how to ask, edit your askings, and receive miracles. Master the subconscious mind through repetitive conditioning. We use the power of affirmations and imprint new powerful beliefs.

Group of 8, 4 x 60 min., 4 consecutive weeks, $100

READING AND LISTENING RECOMMENDATION

Receive Joy presents: Kathryn Gaertner

THE BEAUTIFUL WORD SOLUTION

Receive joy, positivity, and beauty. Learn to use written prayer processes with beautiful words. Beautiful words leverage our well-being. Choose to see beauty everywhere and enjoy beauty every day. Live a glorious future.

$15, 45 pages, ISBN: 978-1-5426757-3-4

DIVINE ENTRAINMENT

Every positive emotion embedded in your memory is an access point to your spirit. The ultimate secret of true prosperity is finding our security through our connection with the divine.

$12, 39 pages ISBN: 978-1-5482791-5-8

THE RECEIVING CYCLE MEDITATION

This Receiving Cycle Meditation CD will help you feel uplifted and even more connected to your higher self. Each track contains guided imagery, relaxing melodies, healing tones, and focus sounds. Receive grace from above as you relax, breathe deeply and listen.

$15, 5 tracks

All of Kathryn Gaertner's products are directly available from Receive Joy.

LIGHT ONE CANDLE AT A TIME

Our experience on Earth is an opportunity for each of us to investigate our inner being and choose to be a light. My desire is for humanity to **be the light** of love, joy, peace, patience, kindness, goodness, faithfulness, gentleness, and self-control as this is the fruit, the pouring fourth, of the Holy Spirit (Galatians 5:22-23).

My wish is for each of us to **be a conscious light** so that we can **light others**, one candle (person) at a time. Let us be conscious of our thoughts and our words. Let us be rightminded so that our light of truth is whole and well as it flows through us and is passed on.

Be the light for God and give a copy of this book to your family members and friends.

Receive Joy asks everyone we meet along our path to share their miraculous stories. We also invite you to share your illuminating miracle stories.

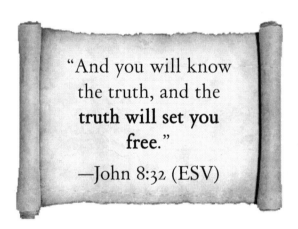

"And you will know the truth, and the **truth will set you free.**"

—John 8:32 (ESV)

OWN A BIBLE

When you happen to require a Bible, go and obtain one; or more than one! Own your personal Bible! Yes, you can download an app; however, there is something magical in seeing and feeling God's inspired Word printed on paper. Thrift stores sell used Bibles for a small price. Every bookstore and online bookseller carries this bestseller.

There are different versions you can choose from. Some have Jesus' Words highlighted in red, others are color-coded by topic.

The Bible comes in different translations. When you are purchasing a Bible for the first time, you may wish to pick a translation that is easy to read. In that case, you may choose the New Living Translation (NLT). The version thought by some to be most accurately translated is the New American Standard Bible (NASB). Bible studies commonly choose the New International Version (NIV). The New King James Version (NKJV) is widely favored. There are many other versions. Select one that you are drawn to. Use your Bible actively—every day of the week. Highlight passages, underline verses, take notes on the pages, post sticky notes. Be familiar with your Bible. Allow it to be a best friend that offers the best advice. Let it talk to you. Let the Living Word inspire you. Gain intimacy with the best book ever written!

Receive Joy uses different Bible versions to demonstrate the power of positive words:

ESV   English Standard Version
KJV   King James Version
NIV   New International Version
NKJV New King James Version
NLT   New Living Translation

To learn more and receive FREE INSPIRATIONS
visit **www.receivejoy.com**
For instant access to Receive Joy's webpage,
Instagram, Facebook and YouTube,
please scan the QR code:

SCAN ME

Enjoy and like recorded Miracle Group Meetings and
more on YouTube.
Subscribe to the Receive Joy channel on YouTube:
https://www.youtube.com/channel/UCCVKbLYsVfs4Vkr1Bl-G3Vg

Like and follow Receive Joy on Facebook:
www.facebook.com/ReceiveJoy

Follow Receive Joy on Instagram:
@receivejoy #receivejoy

Subscribe to our newsletter to continue your receiving of positive awareness.
Please share your email address with us:
ask@receivejoy.com

Call or text to U.S. cell phone number **(239) 450-1240**

We are happy to hear from you and receive your positive feedback, inspiration,
and miracle stories!

With Love and Gratitude,

Notes

Notes

Notes

Notes

Notes

Notes

Notes

Notes

Notes

Notes

Made in the USA
Columbia, SC
13 August 2021

43157566R00093